Insights You Need from
Harvard
Business
Review

CYBERSECURITY

Insights You Need from Harvard Business Review

Business is changing. Will you adapt or be left behind?

Get up to speed and deepen your understanding of the topics that are shaping your company's future with the **Insights You Need from Harvard Business Review** series. Featuring HBR's smartest thinking on fast-moving issues—blockchain, cybersecurity, AI, and more—each book provides the foundational introduction and practical case studies your organization needs to compete today and collects the best research, interviews, and analysis to get it ready for tomorrow.

You can't afford to ignore how these issues will transform the landscape of business and society. The Insights You Need series will help you grasp these critical ideas—and prepare you and your company for the future.

Books in the series include:

Agile

Artificial Intelligence

Blockchain

Cybersecurity

Monopolies and Tech Giants

Strategic Analytics

Insights You Need from
**Harvard
Business
Review**

CYBERSECURITY

Harvard Business Review Press
Boston, Mas sachusetts

10 9 8 7 6 5 4 3 2 1

Library of Congress Cataloging-in-Publication Data

Title: Cybersecurity : the insights you need from Harvard Business Review.
Other titles: Cybersecurity (Harvard Business Review Press) |
    Insights you need from Harvard Business Review.
Description: Boston, Massachusetts : Harvard Business Review Press,
    [2019] | Series: Insights you need from Harvard Business Review |
    Includes bibliographical references and index.
Identifiers: LCCN 2019013638 | ISBN 978-1-63369-828-4
Subjects: LCSH: Computer security. | Business enterprises—Security
    measures.
Classification: LCC QA76.9.A25 C924 2019 | DDC 005.8—dc23
    LC record available at https://lccn.loc.gov/2019013638

ISBN: 978-1-63369-828-4

Contents

Contents

Introduction

WE'RE ALL IN THIS NOW

by Alex Blau

The internet was once just an idea in someone's head. A seemingly unfathomable future where everything and everyone would be connected, and where uninhibited flows of data and information would enable unprecedented advancements in communication, health care, transportation, automation, and commerce. And there would be robots, of course. The world in which we live today is not that far off from the imaginings of those futurists, and because of these technologies the ways in which firms and governments operate have fundamentally changed. Embedded in these cyberpunk dreams were prescient warnings about the potential risks inherent to our interconnected world. Hackers, advanced artificial intelligence, and bad actors in the form of governments and megacorporations posed significant threats to the goings-on of everyday life. Even the most shining cyber utopia can have a sinister underworld.

Today, in our real world, the same technologies that brought so much good have created new and ever-shifting cybersecurity consequences for individuals, firms, and governments. These consequences range from the annoying task of coming up with new and complicated passwords following yet another data breach, to the uncomfortably real risks of a foreign adversary turning off streetlights, shutting down water treatment plants, or even taking over military infrastructure.

While managing risk has historically been assigned to experts and technicians, cybersecurity can no longer be delegated to a small set (or even a large team) of IT professionals. Instead, all of us leaders across all aspects of business operations and government need to understand how cybersecurity plays into our roles and responsibilities, and to keep up with the fluid nature of cybersecurity risks. *Cybersecurity* will help non-experts quickly gain a foundational understanding of the cybersecurity domain. This book covers a number of critical topics that will aid any reader in becoming conversant in current and future cybersecurity issues relevant to your role, organization, and industry, and in understanding how you are both part of your organization's security problem as well as a key player in identifying and managing solutions.

In more and more industries, the gathering of data and digital information on nearly everything, especially customers, is at the center of business operations and strategy. But while petabytes of data can improve operational efficiency and open new opportunities, those larger amounts of data also expose individuals and firms to potential losses. Cyberattacks and data breaches are commonplace, increasing in volume, and becoming costlier by the year. Despite our growing capabilities to thwart most attacks through improvements to security technology and cyber hygiene, targeted breaches have not declined. We need to revise our expectations about our ability to mitigate these risks and accept that breaches are all but inevitable. As customer data becomes more valuable to hackers, and as governments enact regulations that penalize firms for customer data breaches and loss, nearly all firms that have an internet presence and collect information from their customers face increased risks—it's not just about banks and financial service organizations anymore.

This new paradigm requires a different way of thinking, and this book is designed to help non-technical leaders, including executives, board members, and managers in roles ranging from design and marketing, to human resources and accounting, get up to speed on the current state of the field. *Cybersecurity* introduces the basics while going deeper into a set of topics including board and executive involvement, investment and decision making in cybersecurity; the importance of addressing human factors in cybersecurity and why all team members need to play a role; communications and response best practices in the wake of data breaches; active defense and the ethics of "hacking back"; the emerging value of privacy in cybersecurity; cybersecurity considerations for international trade; and the future of artificial intelligence in cybersecurity. These selected articles will help you understand who to consult on critical issues, keep up with your competitors and colleagues, recognize the potential impact for your team, organization, and industry, and think through how your organization will need to evolve to keep up with cybersecurity trends in the future.

This book represents just the beginning. Cybersecurity is still a relatively new field, and one that will continue to shift dynamically with changes to the nascent regulatory environment and as new technologies are developed and advancements occur. Some of these changes will be for the benefit of society at large. For instance, regulations such as the European Union's General Data Protection Regulation (GDPR) have already begun to incentivize firms to take greater precautions and care with customer data, and disincentivize business models that rely on the sale of such data to third parties. However, other changes, such as advancements in artificial intelligence and quantum computing, will pose new and potentially existential threats to businesses and governments that could make our current and best cybersecurity efforts obsolete. Understanding these new risks and opportunities will be critical to the success of firms in the future, as well as the protection of people and society broadly.

The field of cybersecurity isn't just for techno-futurists and digital natives. We've all been brought into this futuristic present whether we like it or not. If we, the global community, have any hope of avoiding a techno-catastrophe and ultimately realizing the great potential of what we've created, each and every one of us needs to recognize that we're all in this together now. We all have a part to play.

Further Reading

If after reading this book you want to dig deeper, I highly recommend the following titles:

LikeWar: The Weaponization of Social Media, by Peter W. Singer and Emerson T. Brooking (Houghton Mifflin Harcourt, 2018)

(Continued)

Cybersecurity and Cyberwar: What Everyone Needs to Know, by Peter W. Singer and Allan Friedman (Oxford University Press, 2014)

Countdown to Zero Day: Stuxnet and the Launch of the World's First Digital Weapon, by Kim Zetter (Crown, 2014)

The Art of Deception: Controlling the Human Element of Security, by Kevin D. Mitnik and William L. Simon (Wiley, 2002)

Move Fast and Break Things: How Facebook, Google, and Amazon Cornered Culture and Undermined Democracy, by Jonathan Taplin (Little, Brown, 2017)

Cyber War: The Next Threat to National Security and What to Do About It, by Richard A. Clarke and Robert Knake (Ecco, 2010)

Future Crimes: Everything Is Connected, Everyone Is Vulnerable and What We Can Do About It, by Marc Goodman (Doubleday, 2015)

INTERNET INSECURITY

by Andy Bochman

H ere's the brutal truth: It doesn't matter how much your organization spends on the latest cyberse- curity hardware, software, training, and staff or whether it has segregated its most essential systems from the rest. If your mission-critical systems are digital and connected in some form or fashion to the internet (even if you think they aren't, it's highly likely they are), they can never be made fully safe. Period.

This matters because digital, connected systems now permeate virtually every sector of the U.S. economy, and the sophistication and activity of adversaries—most notably nation-states, criminal syndicates, and terror- ist groups—have increased enormously in recent years.

Witness the attacks in the United States on Atlanta's municipal government and on a data network shared by four operators of natural-gas pipelines, the theft of data from Equifax, and the global WannaCry and NotPetya malware attacks. In many of the most notorious incidents of recent years, the breached companies thought they had strong cyber defenses.

I am a member of a team at the Idaho National Lab (INL) that has been studying how organizations critical to the U.S. economy and national security can best protect themselves against cyberattacks. We've focused on those that rely on industrial control systems—such as the ones that regulate heat and pressure in electric utilities and oil refineries—and have come up with a solution that flies in the face of all conventional remedies: Identify the functions whose failure would jeopardize your business, isolate them from the internet to the greatest extent possible, reduce their reliance on digital technologies to an absolute minimum, and backstop their monitoring and control with analog devices and trusted human beings. Although our methodology is still in the pilot stage, organizations can apply many elements of the approach now.

Admittedly, this strategy—which isn't feasible for purely information-based businesses—may raise operating costs and reduce efficiency in some cases. But it's the only way to ensure that mission-critical systems can't be successfully attacked by digital means. In this chapter I will share the lab's methodology for identifying such systems. It invariably turns up vulnerable functions or processes that leaders never realized were so vital that their compromise could put the organization out of business. We've applied elements of the methodology at companies and in the U.S. military for the past several years and conducted a highly successful yearlong pilot of the entire approach at Florida Power & Light, one of the largest electric utilities in the United States. A second pilot in one of the U.S. military services is now under way. INL is also exploring ways to take the process mainstream. This will most likely mean partnering with selected engineering services firms and getting them licensed and trained to apply the methodology.

The Existing Threat

In the old days, mechanical pumps, compressors, valves, relays, and actuators did the work in industrial companies. Situational awareness came from analog gauges, and skilled and trusted engineers communicated with headquarters via landline telephone circuits. Other than tampering with the supply chain or co-opting an employee, the only way a saboteur could disrupt operations was to go to the plant and bypass the three physical pillars of security: gates, guards, and guns.

Today operations in 12 of the 16 infrastructure sectors that the U.S. Department of Homeland Security has deemed critical—because their "assets, systems, and networks, whether physical or virtual, are considered so vital to the United States that their incapacitation or destruction would have a debilitating effect on security, national economic security, national public health or safety, or any combination thereof"—depend partially or fully on digital control and safety systems. Although digital technologies bring wonderful new capabilities and efficiencies, they have proved to be highly susceptible to cyberattacks. The systems of large corporations, government agencies, and academic institutions are constantly being prodded for weaknesses by automated probes that are readily available on the dark web; many are free, and others cost hundreds or thousands of dollars (the more expensive ones even come with technical support). They can often be thwarted by cybersecurity best practices, but in reality it is virtually impossible to defend against well-planned, targeted attacks—meticulously conducted over months if not years.

The financial impact of cyberattacks is soaring. Just two in 2017, the ones involving WannaCry and NotPetya, caused damage worth more than $4 billion and $850 million, respectively. The WannaCry attack, which the

United States and the United Kingdom accused North Korea of carrying out, reportedly used tools stolen from the National Security Agency. Exploiting an opening in Windows machines that hadn't installed a Microsoft security patch, it encrypted data; crippled hundreds of thousands of computers in hospitals, schools, businesses, and homes in 150 countries; and demanded a ransom. The NotPetya attack, which Russia is believed to have carried out as part of its campaign to destabilize Ukraine, was conducted through an update to a Ukrainian accounting company's software. It began with an assault on Ukrainian government and computer systems and spread to other parts of the world, with corporate victims including the Danish shipping company Maersk, the pharma firm Merck, the chocolate manufacturer Cadbury, and the advertising behemoth WPP, among many others.

A Growing Vulnerability

The pace of digital transformation continues to accelerate with the growth of automation, the internet of things, cloud processing and storage, and artificial intelligence and machine learning. The propagation of and growing dependency on complex, internet-connected, software-intensive digital technologies carries a serious cybersecurity downside. In a 2014 article published by the Center for a New American Security, Richard J. Danzig, a former secretary of the navy and now a board director at the center, spelled out the paradox posed by digital technologies:

> *Even as they grant unprecedented powers, they also make users less secure. Their communicative capabilities enable collaboration and networking, but in so doing they open doors to intrusion. Their concentration of data and manipulative power vastly improves the efficiency and scale of operations, but this concentration in turn exponentially increases the amount that can be stolen or subverted by a successful attack. The complexity of their hardware and software creates great capability, but this complexity spawns vulnerabilities and lowers the visibility of intrusions . . . In sum, cyber systems nourish us, but at the same time they weaken and poison us.*

The fact is that these technologies are so mind-bogglingly complex that even the vendors who create and know them best don't fully understand their vulnerabilities. Vendors typically sell automation as a way to remove risks posed by fault-prone humans, but it just replaces those risks with others. Information systems now are so complicated that U.S. companies need more than

200 days, on average, just to detect that they have been breached, according to the Ponemon Institute, a center that conducts independent research on privacy, data protection, and information security policy. And most often they don't find the breach themselves; they are notified by third parties.

Despite the ever-expanding number of damaging, high-profile cyberattacks throughout the world, on companies such as Target, Sony Pictures, Equifax, Home Depot, Maersk, Merck, and Saudi Aramco, business leaders have been unable to resist the allure of digital technologies and the many benefits they provide: greater efficiency, lower head counts, the reduction or elimination of human error, quality improvements, opportunities to glean much more information about customers, and the ability to create new offerings. Leaders spend more and more every year on new security solutions and high-priced consultants, continuing with conventional approaches to cybersecurity and hoping for the best. That is wishful thinking.

The Limitations of "Cyber Hygiene"

These conventional approaches—or "hygiene" in the cybersecurity trade—include:

- Creating comprehensive inventories of a company's hardware and software assets

- Buying and deploying the latest defensive hardware and software tools, including endpoint security, firewalls, and intrusion-detection systems

- Regularly training employees to recognize and avoid phishing emails

- Creating "air gaps"—in theory, separating important systems from other networks and the internet—though in practice, there are no true air gaps

- Building a large cybersecurity staff supplemented with various services and service providers to do all of the above

Many organizations adhere to best-practices frameworks such as the National Institute of Standards and Technology's (NIST) cybersecurity framework and the SANS Institute's top 20 security controls. These entail continuously performing hundreds of activities without error. They include mandating that employees use complex passwords and change them frequently, encrypting data in transit, segmenting networks by placing firewalls between them, immediately installing new security patches, limiting the number of people who have access to sensitive systems, vetting suppliers, and so on.

Many CEOs seem to believe that by hewing to cyber-hygiene best practices, they can protect their organizations from grievous harm. The numerous high-profile breaches amply demonstrate the error of this presumption. All the companies previously mentioned had large cybersecurity staffs and were spending significant sums on cybersecurity when they were breached. Cyber hygiene is effective against run-of-the-mill automated probes and amateurish hackers, but not so in addressing the growing number of targeted and persistent threats to critical assets posed by sophisticated adversaries.

In asset-intensive industries such as energy, transportation, and heavy manufacturing, no amount of talent or money can accomplish all the prescribed best practices without error. In fact, most organizations fail at the first of the recommended practices: creating comprehensive inventories of the company's hardware and software assets. That is a huge shortcoming, because you can't secure what you don't even know you have.

Then there are the trade-offs inherent in the best practices. Security upgrades usually require that systems be shut down for installation, but that's not always feasible. For example, utilities, chemical companies, and others that put a premium on the availability and reliability of their industrial processes or systems can't stop them every time a software company issues a new security patch. So they tend to install the patches periodically, in batches, during scheduled downtime, often many months after a patch is released. Another issue is protecting widely dispersed assets. Larger utilities, for example, operate thousands of substations, which often are spread out over thousands of square miles. Refreshing them presents a quandary: If you can access the software via a network to implement updates, a talented adversary may just as easily tap into the network to access the software for nefarious purposes. But if your own employees physically update the software at all those plants, the effort can be prohibitively expensive. And if you subcontract that work to independent outfits, you can't hope to sufficiently vet them all.

Even if the best practices could be implemented perfectly, they would be no match for sophisticated hackers, who are well funded, patient, constantly evolving, and can always find plenty of open doors to walk through. No matter how good your company's hygiene is, a targeted attack will penetrate your networks and systems. It may take the hackers weeks or months, but they will get in.

That's not just my view. Michael Assante, a former chief security officer of American Electric Power and now a leader at the SANS Institute, told me, "Cyber hygiene is helpful for warding off online ankle biters" and "if done perfectly in a utopian world, might thwart 95% of attackers." But in the real world, he said, it registers as "barely a speed bump for sophisticated attackers aiming at a particular target." And in an interview last year with the *Wall Street Journal*, Bob Lord, the former head of security for Yahoo and Twitter, said, "When I talk to corporate security officers, I see a little bit of this fatalism, which is 'I can't defend against the most sophisticated nation-state attack. Therefore, it is a lost game. So I'm not really going to start to think deeply about the problem.'"

One case in point is the 2012 Shamoon virus attack on Saudi Aramco, which had good defenses in place. The attack, which U.S. officials suspect was carried out by Iran, erased data on three-quarters of the oil company's corporate PCs. A more recent attack, in March 2018, was designed to trigger a blast at a Saudi petrochemical plant by interfering with safety controllers. It might have succeeded had the attacker's code not contained an error, according to the *New York Times*. "The attackers not only had to figure out how to get into that system, they had to understand its design well enough to know the layout of the facility—what pipes went where and which valves to turn in order to trigger an explosion," the *Times* wrote.

INL's Radical Idea

It's time to embrace a drastically different approach: a highly selective shift away from full reliance on digital complexity and connectivity. This can be done by identifying the most essential processes and functions and then reducing or eliminating the digital pathways attackers could use to reach them.

The Idaho National Lab has developed a step-by-step approach: its consequence-driven, cyber-informed engineering (CCE) methodology. The objective of CCE is not a one-time risk assessment; rather, it is to permanently change how senior leaders think about and weigh strategic cyber risks to their companies. Although it is still in the pilot stage, we've seen great results. We plan to have CCE fully ramped up in 2019 and to have several services firms licensed to implement the methodology by 2020. But even today, the core precepts of the CCE approach can be adapted by any organization. (The lab has also developed a companion framework: cyber-informed engineering [CIE], which, while similar to CCE in many respects, describes methods for integrating cyber risk mitigations across the entire engineering life cycle.)

The methodology comprises four steps that should

be performed in a highly collaborative fashion by the following:

- A CCE master—now someone from the INL, but in the future people at engineering-services firms trained by the INL

- All the leaders responsible for regulatory compliance, litigation, and mitigating risks: the CEO, the chief operating officer, the chief financial officer, the chief risk officer, the general counsel, and the chief security officer (CSO)

- The people who oversee core operational functions

- Safety system experts and the operators and engineers most familiar with the processes on which the company most depends

- Cyber experts and process engineers who know how systems and equipment can be misused

For a number of these people, the process will be stressful. For example, the exposure of heretofore unknown enterprise-level risks is bound to initially make the CSO squirm. But often that is not fair. No CSO can hope to fully prepare a company for an attack by a highly resourced adversary.

1. Identify "crown jewel" processes

The work begins with what the INL calls *consequence prioritization*: the generation of possible catastrophic scenarios, or high-consequence events. This involves identifying functions or processes whose failure would be so damaging that it would threaten the company's very survival. Examples include an attack on transformers that would stop an electric utility from distributing electricity—or on compressor stations that would prevent a natural gas distribution company from delivering to its customers—for a month. Other examples include a targeted attack on the safety systems in a chemical plant or an oil refinery that would cause pressure to exceed limits, leading to an explosion that could kill or injure hundreds or thousands of people, generate lawsuits seeking ruinous damages, wreak havoc with the company's market cap, and cost its leaders their jobs.

Analysts familiar with how sophisticated cyber adversaries act help the team envision what prospective attackers' end goals might be. By answering questions such as "What would *you* do if you wanted to disrupt your processes or ruin your company?" and "What are the first facilities *you* would go after the hardest?" the team can identify the targets whose disruption would be the most destructive and the most feasible and develop scenarios involving them for discussion by the C-suite. Depending on the size of the company, this step may take a few weeks to a few months.

2. Map the digital terrain

The next task, which typically takes a full week but may take longer, is mapping all the hardware, software, and communications technologies and the supporting people and processes (including third-party suppliers and services) in the company-ending scenarios. It entails laying out the steps of production, documenting in robust detail all the places where control and automation systems are employed, and capturing all the necessary physical or data inputs into the function or process. These connections are potential pathways for attackers, and companies often are not aware of all of them.

Existing maps of these elements never fully match the reality. Questions such as "Who touches your equipment?" and "How does information move through your networks and how do you protect it?" will always turn up surprises. For example, the team may discover from a network architect or the control engineer that a vital system is connected not just to the operational systems network but to the business network that deals with accounts payable and receivable, payment systems, customer-information systems, and—by extension—the internet. By asking the person responsible for managing vendors, the team might learn that the supplier of this system maintains a direct wireless connection to it in order to perform remote analysis and diagnostics. A safety-system supplier may say that it can't directly communicate with the equipment, but a careful examination of the mechanics and update processes may reveal that it can. Any such discovery is an aha moment for the team.

3. Illuminate the likely attack paths

Then, using a variant of a methodology developed by Lockheed Martin, the team identifies the shortest, most likely paths attackers would take to reach the targets identified in step 1.[1] These paths are ranked by their degree of difficulty. The CCE master and other outside experts, including people with access to sensitive information about attackers and their methods, play the lead roles in this phase. They share information gleaned from government sources about attacks on similar systems around the world. Additional company input regarding safety systems, the firm's capabilities and procedures for responding to cyberthreats, and so on help the team finalize a list of attack paths, which is used in step 4 to prioritize remediation actions for senior leaders to consider.

4. Generate options for mitigation and protection

Now it's time to come up with options for engineering out highest-consequence cyber risks. If there are 10 pathways to a target but they all pass through one particular node, that's obviously a great place to install a tripwire—a closely monitored sensor that would alert a fast-response team of defenders at the first sign of trouble.

Some remedies are surprisingly easy and inexpensive to implement: for example, a software-free, hardwired vibration sensor that will slow down or trip a unit that has been given malicious digital instructions that might cause it to damage or destroy itself. Others take more time and money, such as keeping a redundant but not identical backup system ready to continue a crucial function, even if in a somewhat degraded state. Although many remedies will have no negative impact on operational efficiency and business opportunities, others might. So a company's leaders will ultimately have to decide how to proceed on the basis of what risks they can accept, must avoid, can transfer, or should try to mitigate.

If a selected process simply must have a digital channel for monitoring or sending control signals, the goal should be to keep the number of digital pathways to and from the critical process at an absolute minimum to make spotting abnormal traffic easier. In addition, a company might add a device to protect a system should it receive digital commands that would cause a catastrophic event—a mechanical valve or switch, for example, that would prevent the pressure or the temperature from exceeding specified parameters. And sometimes a company might want to reinsert trusted people into the activity—to monitor a mechanical thermometer or pressure gauge, for instance, to ensure that the digital devices are telling the true story. If your company has not suffered a serious cyber incident, the notion of disconnecting as much as possible, installing old-fashioned mechanical devices, and inserting humans in automated functions might sound like a regressive business decision. Instead it should be reframed as a proactive risk-management decision. It may decrease efficiency, but if the somewhat higher cost radically reduces the likelihood of a disaster that your current methods can't protect against, it is the smart move.

It's not hard to imagine CEOs and COOs reading through this process with skepticism. In any change-management project, moving hearts and minds from ideas they've hewn to for decades is a massive challenge. Anticipate resistance, especially early on. Divulging so much information about your company and admitting to weaknesses you either didn't know about or didn't want to think about will be psychologically taxing. Later phases will challenge engineers' fortitude as their systems and practices are pored over for weaknesses. Make sure team members feel safe during even the hardest evaluations of your systems. In the end, the detailed information about adversaries' approaches and what they could achieve—showing how it could happen to you—will be a revelation. Even the most resistant team members should climb on board when they recognize the risks and the best way to mitigate them.

What You Can Do Today

Learn to think like your adversaries. You might go as far as to build an internal team charged with continually assessing the strength of your defenses by trying to reach critical targets. The team should include experts in the processes in question, control and safety systems, and operational networks.

Even if you can maintain consistently high levels of cyber hygiene, you must prepare for a breach. The best way to do that is to create a cyber safety culture similar to those that exist at elite chemical factories and nuclear power plants. Every employee, from the most senior to the most junior, should be aware of the importance of reacting quickly when a computer system or a machine in their care starts acting abnormally: It might be an equipment malfunction, but it might also indicate a cyberattack.

Finally, a Plan B should be ready for implementation if and when you and your team lose confidence in systems that support your most critical functions. It should be designed to allow your company to continue essential operations, even if at a reduced level. Ideally, the backup system should not rely on digital technologies and should not be connected to a network—particularly the internet. But at a minimum, it should not exactly replicate the one in question, for an obvious reason: If attackers were able to breach the original, they'll be able to easily invade one identical to it.

. . .

Every organization that depends on digital technologies and the internet is vulnerable to a devastating cyberattack. Not even the best cyber hygiene will stop Russia, North Korea, and highly skilled, well-resourced criminal and terrorist groups. The only way to protect your business is to take, where you can, what may look like a technological step backward but in reality is a smart engineering step forward. The goal is to reduce, if not eliminate, the dependency of critical functions on digital technologies and their connections to the internet. The sometimes-higher cost will be a bargain when compared with the potentially devastating price of business as usual.

TAKEAWAYS

While digital technologies bring new capabilities and efficiencies to modern industry, they also bring new security challenges. It doesn't matter how much your company invests in traditional cybersecurity defenses such as hardware, software, and training: If your company's critical systems are digital and connected to the internet, they can never be fully secured.

✓ Even if best practices are perfectly implemented, hackers are sophisticated, well-funded, patient, evolving, and crafty enough to find ways in.

✓ Identify the processes or functions where a breach could jeopardize your business and isolate them from the internet as much as possible, minimize their reliance on digital technology, and monitor and control them with analog devices or trusted humans.

✓ Extensively inventory all the hardware, software, and communications technologies, along with the processes and people that support them, in that jeopardy scenario.

✓ Learn to think like your adversaries and identify the likely paths attackers would follow to reach their targets.

✓ Create a culture where every employee is on watch for abnormal behavior from computer systems or machines and knows to react quickly.

NOTE

1. Michael J. Assante and Robert M. Lee, "The Industrial Control System Cyber Kill Chain," SANS Institute paper, October 2105, https://www.sans.org/reading-room/whitepapers/ICS/paper/36297; and Lockheed Martin website, "The Cyber Kill Chain," https://www.lockheedmartin.com/en-us/capabilities/cyber/cyber-kill-chain.html.

Adapted from content posted on hbr.org, May 15, 2018 (product #BG1803).

2

SECURITY TRENDS BY THE NUMBERS

by Scott Berinato and Matt Perry

T o understand the discouraging state of cybersecurity, first consider the stats in figure 2-1, from surveys conducted with companies around the globe in 2017. Respondents were asked about the incidence in their firms of targeted attacks—assaults with the potential to penetrate network defenses and damage or extract valuable assets (as opposed to the countless low-level nefarious activities that are more nuisance than threat). They also reported on breaches—attacks that get through.

According to a similar survey in 2018 (figure 2-2), the proportion of targeted attacks that were thwarted has

FIGURE 2-1

Average annual number of targeted attacks and breaches per company

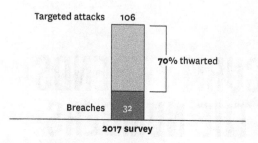

Source: Accenture, "2018 State of Cyber Resilience: Gaining Ground on the Cyber Attacker"

risen to 87%. That might sound like good news, but the number of attacks also continues to increase.

And when you take the data in figure 2-3 into account it becomes clear that companies are spending more and more just to tread water. Firms are seeing roughly the same number of breaches, on average. And experts believe that number will not fall substantially, because attacks will keep increasing. Moreover, they worry that breaches will affect higher-impact targets and have more far-reaching consequences. Spending, too, is likely to keep rising, owing to the intensifying use of preventative measures and the increasing costs of breaches.

FIGURE 2-2

Even though we're thwarting more attacks, we're not preventing more breaches

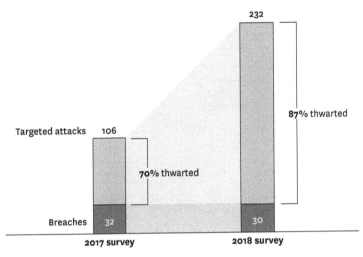

Source: Accenture, "2018 State of Cyber Resilience: Gaining Ground on the Cyber Attacker"

In this chapter we offer a visual exploration of the state of cybersecurity, with charts drawn from three highly respected industry reports. Verizon's "2018 Data Breach Investigations Report" analyzes more than 53,000 cyber-security incidents (events that potentially expose data) and 2,216 breaches (incidents resulting in the confirmed disclosure of data) in 65 countries. Accenture's "2018 State of Cyber Resilience" is based on surveys of 4,600

FIGURE 2-3

Average cost of cybercrime per company (US$M)

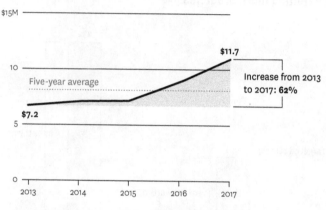

Source: Accenture and Ponemon Institute, "2017 Cost of Cyber Crime Study: Insights on the Security Investments That Make a Difference"

executives at $1 billion-plus companies in 19 industries across 15 countries. Its "2017 Cost of Cyber Crime Study," conducted with the Ponemon Institute, draws on responses from 254 companies in seven countries. Although definitive data on cybersecurity events is hard to come by, given the often-elusive nature of the threat, together these reports provide a detailed picture of the state of play.

The data reveals a dual reality. On the one hand, things haven't changed: Attacks occur constantly and employ many of the same technical approaches that have been used for years. On the other hand, things have changed radically: More attacks take place now than ever before. And they're getting more vicious: We're seeing more assaults on critical infrastructure and a veritable onslaught of "ransomware," which locks users out of their data or technology until they pay up.

Here's what we know about cybersecurity today.

Who's Getting In?

Roughly a quarter of all breaches come from internal sources—but most industries deviate from the average (figure 2-4). In those involving highly sensitive and valuable information—health care, public administration, and professional, technical, and scientific services—the proportion of internal troublemakers is higher, whereas public-facing industries, restaurants, and stores see much more activity from the outside.

How Often Are They Getting In?

In a few highly vulnerable industries, hackers get in more often than not. But in most, multiple attacks are needed to achieve a breach (figure 2-5).

FIGURE 2-4

Attacks come mostly from outsiders

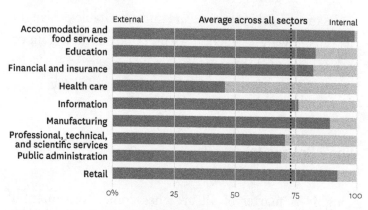

Note: Some external totals include partners and/or multiple parties.
Source: Accenture, "2018 Data Breach Investigations Report"

The ratio of incidents to breaches in an industry says much about its vulnerability. Accommodation and food services is one of the most vulnerable targets: It averages 11 breaches for every unsuccessful attack, although the payoff for breaking in is often lower than in other industries. The public sector is under massive attack, with the highest number of incidents of the industries studied. But most of them fail: For every 74 unsuccessful attacks, it sees just one breach.

FIGURE 2-5

Attacks still fail more often than they succeed

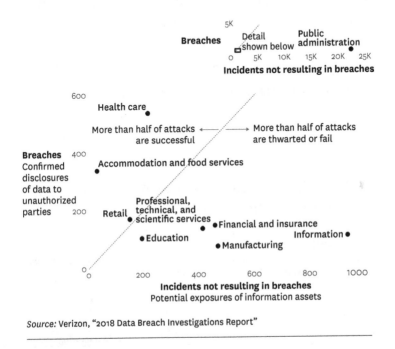

Source: Verizon, "2018 Data Breach Investigations Report"

What Are They Getting?

Despite all the work that's gone into protecting user data and credit card data in recent years, those are the most commonly nabbed assets (figure 2-6). Other information-based targets not reflected here, such as contracts, RFPs (requests for proposals), and control systems, are experiencing more breaches than in the past, but user data and credit card data remain the most popular and vulnerable targets—suggesting that all our defenses haven't helped as much as they should have.

Industries in which breaches overwhelmingly involve a single type of information (medical, accommodation and food services) can hone their defenses, because the

FIGURE 2-6

Personal information and payment information are the most commonly compromised targets

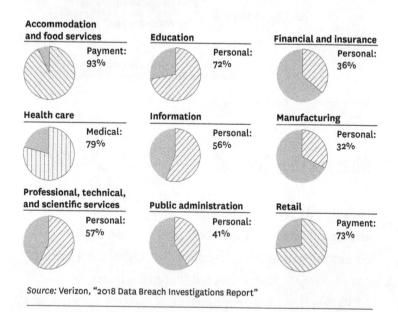

Accommodation and food services
Payment: 93%

Education
Personal: 72%

Financial and insurance
Personal: 36%

Health care
Medical: 79%

Information
Personal: 56%

Manufacturing
Personal: 32%

Professional, technical, and scientific services
Personal: 57%

Public administration
Personal: 41%

Retail
Payment: 73%

Source: Verizon, "2018 Data Breach Investigations Report"

risk is well defined; the bad guys are almost always after the same thing. But industries that have multiple targets, with no one target accounting for a majority of breaches (financial, manufacturing), need a more flexible risk-mitigation strategy, one that will equip them to fight on several fronts.

Different industries have different pathways by which enemies can enter the networks—but note how frequently web apps are implicated in successful attacks (figure 2-7). Looking at an industry's top three sources of incidents (bullet points) against the top three sources of breaches (in bold and black) tells us one of two things:

1. If the top sources of incidents and breaches are the same, those things are heavily targeted, and companies know it—but adversaries are succeeding anyway. Something is amiss.

2. If the top sources of incidents and breaches differ, companies have gotten good at defending on some fronts (where incidents are high but breaches aren't) but have blind spots on others (where breaches are high relative to incidents).

FIGURE 2-7

What hackers attack most often, and what they attack most successfully, aren't always the same

Major sources of breaches are in bold and black; major sources of incidents are (■) bulleted.

Accommodation and food services

Card skimmer
■ Crimeware
Cyber espionage
Denial of service
Lost/stolen asset
■ **Point of sale** →
Privilege misuse
Web app ⎯⎯⎯→
■ **Everything else** →
Misc. errors

96% of all breaches

Education

Card skimmer
Crimeware
Cyber espionage
■ Denial of service
Lost/stolen asset
Point of sale
Privilege misuse
■ **Web app**
■ **Everything else**
Misc. errors

76%

Financial and insurance

■ **Card skimmer**
■ Crimeware
Cyber espionage
■ Denial of service
Lost/stolen asset
Point of sale
Privilege misuse
Web app
■ Everything else
Misc. errors

61%

Health care

Card skimmer
■ Crimeware
Cyber espionage
Denial of service
Lost/stolen asset
Point of sale
■ **Privilege misuse**
Web app
Everything else
■ **Misc. errors**

71%

Information

Card skimmer
Crimeware
Cyber espionage
■ Denial of service
Lost/stolen asset
Point of sale
Privilege misuse
■ **Web app**
■ **Everything else**
Misc. errors

92%

Manufacturing

Card skimmer
■ Crimeware
■ **Cyber espionage**
■ Denial of service
Lost/stolen asset
Point of sale
Privilege misuse
Web app
Everything else
Misc. errors

76%

Professional, technical, and scientific services

Card skimmer
■ Crimeware
■ Cyber espionage
■ Denial of service
Lost/stolen asset
Point of sale
Privilege misuse
Web app
■ **Everything else**
Misc. errors

64%

Public administration

Card skimmer
■ Crimeware
Cyber espionage
Denial of service
■ Lost/stolen asset
Point of sale
■ **Privilege misuse**
Web app
Everything else
Misc. errors

59%

Retail

■ **Card skimmer**
Crimeware
Cyber espionage
■ Denial of service
Lost/stolen asset
Point of sale
Privilege misuse
■ **Web app**
Everything else
Misc. errors

80%

Note: Professional, technical, and scientific services has four bulleted items because of a tie.
Source: Verizon, "2018 Data Breach Investigations Report"

FIGURE 2-8

Average cost of cybercrime per company in selected countries (US$M)

Source: Accenture and Ponemon Institute, "2017 Cost of Cyber Crime Study: Insights on the Security Investments That Make a Difference"

Four Ways to Look at Costs

The simplest way to look at costs is that they're always going up, whether through investments in defense or spending to recover from breaches (figure 2-8).

It's no surprise that the cost of cybercrime is rising around the world. The steepness of the year-over-year increases in Germany and the United States suggests that those countries hold the most appealing—to hackers—combination of value and vulnerability.

FIGURE 2-9

Average annualized cost of cybercrime by sector, worldwide (US$M)

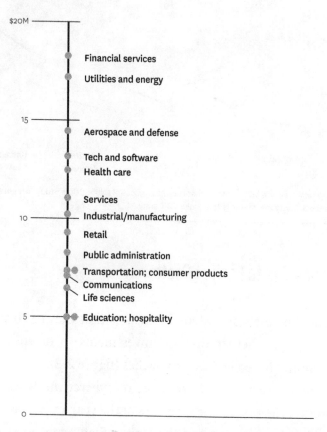

Source: Accenture and Ponemon Institute, "2017 Cost of Cyber Crime Study: Insights on the Security Investments That Make a Difference"

Looking at costs by sector, a few things stand out (figure 2-9). The cost of cybercrime for utilities and energy companies is high in part because of that industry's risk profile: A breach could have immediate and potentially life-threatening consequences. Public sector costs are relatively low, but the sheer volume of attacks means that they are likely to rise significantly, especially as state-level espionage increases.

From 2015 to 2017, as shown in figure 2-10, spending on detection and containment rose by about 5%— and breach prevention rates improved. But as figure 2-11 shows, revenue losses haven't fallen commensurately.

FIGURE 2-10

Share of costs per type of activity

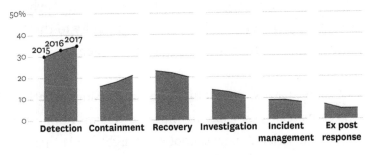

Source: Accenture and Ponemon Institute, "2017 Cost of Cyber Crime Study: Insights on the Security Investments That Make a Difference"

FIGURE 2-11

Share of costs per consequence of attack

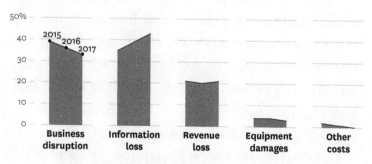

Source: Accenture and Ponemon Institute, "2017 Cost of Cyber Crime Study: Insights on the Security Investments That Make a Difference"

Business disruptions now cost less than they used to; we're getting better at maintaining uptime despite the steady drumbeat of attacks. But the cost of information losses has risen steeply. This is the great paradox of cybersecurity: Although we've improved our ability to thwart attacks, that hasn't reduced the damage when attacks do succeed.

Given all this, companies should consider whether the gains realized by having multiple systems online are worth the risks. A new school of thought holds that it's time to unplug critical systems whose breaches could have dire consequences. Yes, companies would "pay" in terms of convenience and efficiency—but would that price exceed the ever-climbing cost of fending off attacks without making a dent in breaches?

TAKEAWAYS

The state of cybersecurity is pretty discouraging. This collection of charts, created using data from three highly respected industry reports, shows just how bleak the full picture is:

✓ Systems are constantly under attack by hackers employing technical approaches that have been used for years.

✓ Organizations are thwarting more attacks, but more attacks (and more vicious attacks) are taking place now than ever before.

✓ What we know about attacks: Most still come from external sources; they fail more often than they succeed; the most common targets are personal and payment information.

Adapted from content posted on hbr.org, May 23, 2018 (product #BG1803).

3

WHY BOARDS AREN'T DEALING WITH CYBERTHREATS

by J. Yo-Jud Cheng and Boris Groysberg

One of the greatest challenges facing boards today is the one directors feel least prepared for: cybersecurity. In previous work we found that cybersecurity ranked as a top political issue for corporate directors, trailing only the economy and the regulatory environment. Directors acknowledge cybersecurity as an urgent global issue, but they are failing to make the connection between the pervasiveness of cyberthreats and their companies' vulnerabilities. When we asked them to describe their levels of concern and readiness for various risks to their companies, cybersecurity took a back seat to worries about regulatory and reputational risks, which directors were more adequately prepared to deal with. Just 38% of directors reported having a high level of concern about cybersecurity risks, and an even smaller proportion said they were prepared for these risks (figure 3-1). In the words of one director, "Cybersecurity is a big issue, but there is a broad spectrum of risk in this business, so it is a key factor among several."

When directors evaluated the factors that could limit their company's ability to achieve its strategic objectives, cybersecurity issues were overshadowed by more salient concerns like attracting and retaining top talent, the regulatory environment, and global competitive threats (figure 3-2).

These findings confirm that directors simply aren't internalizing the extensive, long-term damage an attack could inflict on their organizations. Why the disconnect between the global- and company-level views? Using a comprehensive survey of more than 5,000 directors in over 60 countries, conducted in partnership with WomenCorporateDirectors Foundation, Spencer Stuart, and independent researcher Deborah Bell, we found two main reasons: Boards lack the processes and the expertise they need to surface, evaluate, and address cyberthreats.

FIGURE 3-1

Most board directors aren't highly concerned about or ready for cyberthreats

Percentage that indicated a "great" or "very great" level of concern/readiness

Q: What is your **level of concern** regarding the following areas of risk to the company?

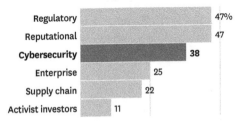

Regulatory	47%
Reputational	47
Cybersecurity	38
Enterprise	25
Supply chain	22
Activist investors	11

Q: What is your **level of readiness** regarding the following areas of risk to the company?

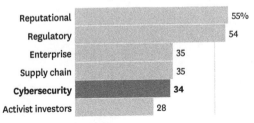

Reputational	55%
Regulatory	54
Enterprise	35
Supply chain	35
Cybersecurity	34
Activist investors	28

Number of participants: 340

FIGURE 3-2

Few board directors view cybersecurity as a strategic threat

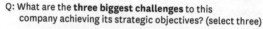

Q: What are the **three biggest challenges** to this company achieving its strategic objectives? (select three)

Attracting and retaining top talent	41%
Regulatory environment	38
Competitive threats: global	32
Competitive threats: domestic	30
Innovation	30
Low or changing consumer demand	21
Technology trends	21
Risk management	14
Levels of debt	12
Cybersecurity	8
Compensation	7
Supply chain risk	7
Rising cost of materials and commodities	6
Activist shareholders	5
Other	10

Number polled: 2,938

Inadequate Processes

Most boards have robust processes for addressing their most pressing responsibilities, such as financial planning and compliance. But when we asked specifically about

FIGURE 3-3

Most board cybersecurity processes fall short, according to directors

Percentage that rated each process as "above average" or "excellent"

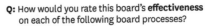

Q: How would you rate this board's **effectiveness** on each of the following board processes?

Process	%
Staying current on company	70%
Compliance	69
Board composition	67
Financial planning	66
Staying current on industry	64
Executive sessions	60
Overall board performance	59
Monitoring strategic decisions	59
Investor/shareholder relations	58
Strategic planning	56
Creating effective board structure	55
Risk management	55
Time management	52
Evaluation of CEO	51
Compensation	45
Mergers and acquisitions	45
Innovation	42
Technology	42
Global expansion	40
CEO succession planning	36
HR/talent management	35
Evaluation of individual directors	34
Cybersecurity	24

Number of participants: 3,183

processes related to cybersecurity issues, such as regular discussions about cyber risks (with or without cybersecurity specialists) and management reviews of contingency plans for a data breach, directors gave their boards low marks (figure 3-3). Only 24% rated those processes as "above average" or "excellent." In fact, among the 23 processes we asked about, directors ranked the ones related to cybersecurity dead last.

The strength of these processes also varied by industry: Boards in the IT and telecom sectors led the field, with 42% reporting strong measures; in the materials and industrials sectors fewer than one in five directors could say the same. In the health care industry, a common target for data breaches, and one that has proven to be particularly vulnerable, 79% of respondents said their organizations lack robust cybersecurity processes.

Lack of Expertise

When we asked directors about the board duties they struggle with, issues of risk and security were the challenges they mentioned most (figure 3-4). The main problem, they said, was that they simply don't have the expertise. One director pointed to "a lack of understanding of the issue and an unwillingness to make room

FIGURE 3-4

Cybersecurity is the biggest challenge for board directors

Q: Which of the following do you find **challenging** in your role as a director on this board? (select all that apply)

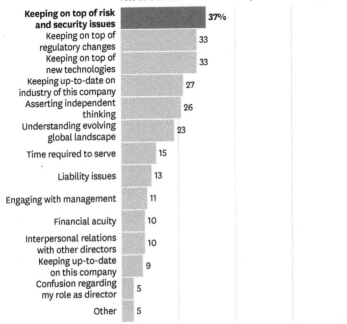

Keeping on top of risk and security issues — 37%
Keeping on top of regulatory changes — 33
Keeping on top of new technologies — 33
Keeping up-to-date on industry of this company — 27
Asserting independent thinking — 26
Understanding evolving global landscape — 23
Time required to serve — 15
Liability issues — 13
Engaging with management — 11
Financial acuity — 10
Interpersonal relations with other directors — 10
Keeping up-to-date on this company — 9
Confusion regarding my role as director — 5
Other — 5

Number of participants: 2,791

for those with new thinking and understanding of the issue." Another said, "There is too much responsibility placed on boards to oversee areas they don't have much experience in, that is, cybersecurity."

A Real Strategic Threat

Boards neglect cybersecurity issues at their peril. An IBM study estimated that the average cost of a data breach is around $4 million.[1] Cisco, in a recent study, noted that targeted companies suffer substantial losses of revenue, customers, and business opportunities.[2] Clearly, these attacks can't be viewed as an abstract external threat. Boards have to embrace the facts and adjust their thinking: Cybersecurity threats are universal, and board members have to take ownership of these risks. The topic should be discussed regularly in all boardrooms, regardless of industry, region, or company size.

Boards can take concrete steps to prioritize cybersecurity issues. One director suggested that directors start by "asking questions and determining whether appropriate processes are in place." Boards can hold executive management accountable for evaluating current cybersecurity risks and maintaining response plans by making cybersecurity debriefings a regular agenda item at board meetings. They can advocate for investments in data security and infrastructure within their organizations, and they can encourage executive management to bring in external experts if needed (boards can bring in their own experts, too, either as consultants or as full board members). These types of investments should be viewed as vital to the organization's risk-management functions and long-term strategy, and they need to be reviewed on a continual basis. As one director told us, "In light of the threats, this issue should be examined in a way that is broader than a risk considered by the audit committee."

The scope of cybersecurity threats will only continue to grow. By being more proactive about cybersecurity issues, directors can play an essential role in safeguarding their organization's stability and supporting future growth.

TAKEAWAYS

Boards don't focus enough on cybersecurity issues. Here's why, and here's what they can do about it:

- ✓ Most boards lack robust processes for regularly discussing cyber risks and reviewing contingency plans for a data breach.

- ✓ Directors feel they lack the expertise needed to address risk and security issues.

✓ Boards should embrace the fact that cybersecurity threats are universal and that they need to take ownership of these risks.

✓ Boards can prioritize and address cybersecurity issues by adopting several practices, including:

- Raising cybersecurity-related questions, even if they don't know the answers

- Making cybersecurity debriefings a regular agenda item at board meetings

- Advocating for investments in data security and risk management infrastructure within the organization

- Bringing in external cybersecurity experts as consultants or full board members

NOTES

1. IBM and Ponemon Institute, "2018 Cost of a Data Breach Study by Ponemon," https://www.ibm.com/security/data-breach.

2. Cisco, "Cisco 2017 Annual Cybersecurity Report: Chief Security Officers Reveal True Cost of Breaches and the Actions Organizations Are Taking," January 31, 2017, https://newsroom.cisco.com/press-release-content?type=webcontent&articleId=1818259.

Adapted from content posted on hbr.org, February 22, 2017 (product #H03GZ7).

THE BEHAVIORAL ECONOMICS OF WHY EXECUTIVES UNDERINVEST IN CYBERSECURITY

by Alex Blau

D etermining the ROI for any cybersecurity investment, from staff training to AI-enabled authentication managers, can best be described as an enigma
shrouded in mystery. The digital threat landscape changes
constantly, and it's very difficult to know the probability

of any given attack succeeding—or how big the potential losses might be. Even the known costs, such as penalties for data breaches in highly regulated industries like health care, are a small piece of the ROI calculation. In the absence of good data, decision makers must use something less than perfect to weigh the options: their judgment.

But insights from behavioral economics and psychology show that human judgment is often biased in predictably problematic ways. In the case of cybersecurity, some decision makers use the wrong mental models to help them determine how much investment is necessary and where to invest. For example, they may think about cyber defense as a fortification process—if you build strong firewalls, with well-manned turrets, you'll be able to see the attacker from a mile away. Or they may assume that complying with a security framework like NIST (National Institute of Standards and Technology) or FISMA (Federal Information Security Modernization Act) is sufficient security—just check all the boxes and you can keep pesky attackers at bay. They may also fail to consider the counterfactual thinking—*We didn't have a breach this year, so we don't need to ramp up investment*—when in reality they probably either got lucky this year or are unaware that a bad actor is lurking in their system, waiting to strike.

The problem with these mental models is that they treat cybersecurity as a finite problem that can be solved, rather than as the ongoing process that it is. No matter how fortified a firm may be, hackers, much like water, will find the cracks in the wall. That's why cybersecurity efforts have to focus on risk *management*, not risk *mitigation*. But this pessimistic outlook makes for a very tough sell. How can security executives get around the misguided thinking that leads to underinvestment, and secure the resources they need?

My behavioral science research and design firm, ideas42, has been interviewing experts across the cybersecurity space and conducting extensive research to identify human behavioral challenges at the levels of engineers, end users, IT administrators, and executives. We've uncovered insights about why people put errors into code, fail to install software updates, and poorly manage access permissions. (We delve into these challenges in *Deep Thought: A Cybersecurity Story*, a research-based novella.) Our findings point to steps that security executives and other cybersecurity professionals can take to work around CEOs' human biases and motivate decision makers to invest more in cyber infrastructure.

Appeal to the emotions of financial decision makers

The way that information is conveyed to us has a huge effect on how we receive and act on it. For cybersecurity professionals, it's intuitive to describe cyber risk in terms of the integrity and availability of data, or with quantifiable metrics like packet loss, but these concepts aren't likely to resonate with decision makers who think about risk very differently. Instead, cybersecurity professionals should take into account people's tendency to overweight information that portrays consequences vividly and tugs at their emotions. To leverage this *affect bias,* security professionals should explain cyber risk by using clear narratives that connect to risk areas that high-level decision makers are familiar with and already care deeply about. For example, your company's risk areas may include customer data loss as well as the regulatory costs and PR fallout that can affect the company's reputation. It's not just about data corruption—it's also about how the bad data will reduce operational efficiency and bring production lines to a standstill.

Replace your CEO's mental model with new success metrics

Everyone uses mental models to distill complexity into something manageable. Having the *wrong* mental model about what a cybersecurity program is supposed to do can be the difference between a thwarted attack and a significant breach. Some CEOs may think that security investments are for building an infrastructure, that creating a fortified castle is all that's needed to keep a company safe. With this mental picture, the goals of a financial decision maker will always be oriented toward risk mitigation instead of risk management.

To get around this, chief information security officers (CISOs) should work with boards and financial decision makers to reframe metrics for success in terms of the number of vulnerabilities that are found and fixed. No cybersecurity system will ever be impenetrable, so working to find the cracks will shift leaders' focus from building the right *system* to building the right *process*. Counterintuitively, a firm's security team uncovering more vulnerabilities should be considered a positive sign. All systems have bugs, and all humans can be hacked, so treating vulnerabilities as shortcomings will create an unintended incentive for an internal security team to hide them. Recognize that the stronger the security processes and team capabilities are, the more vulnerabilities they'll discover (and be able to fix).

Survey your peers to help curb overconfidence

Overconfidence is a pervasive bias, and it can be a big problem if it clouds leaders' judgment about cybersecurity investment. Our research found that many C-level executives believe that their own investments in cybersecurity are sufficient but that few of their peers are investing enough (a belief that, given how widespread it is, can't possibly be true). One way that CISOs can overcome a CEO's overconfidence is to compare the company's performance with a baseline from similar firms—in other words, confront the problem head-on. You can accomplish this by regularly polling CISOs and executives about how well organizations in your industry are managing cybersecurity infrastructure, prompting them to be as specific as possible about what they are doing well and what they're not, and asking those same CISOs to help determine how well your own firm is doing. This way, CISOs can provide clearer information to CEOs about how they are actually performing relative to their industry peers.

"You are the weakest link"

In her essay "Regarding the Pain of Others," Susan Sontag wrote, "To photograph is to frame, and to frame is to exclude." Human attention functions quite similarly. People concentrate on certain aspects of information in their environment while ignoring others; what a CEO chooses to invest in can be thought of in a similar light. For instance, in the wake of a newsworthy hack, CEOs may push their teams to ramp up investment in cyber infrastructure to protect against external threats. But in doing so they may be inattentive to unwitting internal threats that may be just as costly—employees clicking on bad links or falling for phishing attacks.

How can a CISO work around a decision maker's inattention? No one likes to be embarrassed, but negative feedback can sometimes be an effective remedy for inattention. Security teams should regularly try to break their own systems through penetration testing, and the CEO should be the biggest target. After all, that's how outside hackers would see it. By making the CEO the victim of an internally initiated (and safe) attack, it might be possible to draw their attention to potential risks that already exist and motivate leaders to increase their investment in cyber infrastructure.

If the focus of cybersecurity programs continues to be on designing better technologies to combat the growing menace of cyberattacks, we'll continue to neglect the most important aspect of security—the person in the middle. By turning the lens of behavioral science onto cybersecurity challenges, CISOs can identify new ways to approach old problems, and maybe improve their budgets at the same time.

TAKEAWAYS

Decision makers who see cybersecurity as a finite problem to be solved, rather than an ongoing process that needs constant updating and renewal, need new mental models to determine how much and where to invest in cybersecurity:

✓ Cybersecurity professionals should leverage affect bias—the tendency to overweight information that vividly portrays consequences and appeals to emotions—by using stories that connect to risk areas that high-level decision makers already care about, such as customer data loss or regulatory costs.

✓ Reframe metrics for success: focus on building the right *process* instead of the right *system*. View the number of vulnerabilities the security team uncovers as a victory, not a failure.

✓ Curb overconfidence by having the CISO provide information about how the company is doing relative to industry peers.

✓ Target your CEO through an internally initiated (and safe) attack to draw their attention to existing potential risks and to motivate leaders to increase their investment in infrastructure.

Adapted from content posted on hbr.org, June 7, 2017 (product #H03PFQ).

5

WHY THE ENTIRE C-SUITE NEEDS TO USE THE SAME METRICS FOR CYBER RISK

by Jason J. Hogg

W hen it comes to cybersecurity, the chains of communication that exist within an organization, if they exist at all, are often a mess. Multiple conversations about cyber risks are happening across a multitude of divisions in isolation. At the same time, members of the C-suite are measuring their potential impact using different metrics—financial, regulatory, technical, operational—leading to conflicting assessments. CEOs must address these disconnects by creating a culture that promotes open communication and transparency about vulnerabilities and collaboration to address the exposures.

Organizations of all sizes across all sectors are experiencing an exponential increase in their exposure to cyber risk. The number of endpoints that need protecting is exploding as consumers demand more digital interactions and smart devices. (In their 2019 Cybersecurity Almanac, Cisco and Cybersecurity Ventures predict the number of connected devices on the internet will exceed 50 billion by 2020.) Adversaries have evolved from individual bad actors to highly capable organized crime groups and nation-states. The regulatory landscape is increasingly shifting and, at times, conflicting at local, national, and international levels. High-profile cyberattacks—ranging from the one suffered by Sony Pictures in 2014 to the global ransomware attacks that occurred in 2016—highlight the huge financial and reputational stakes.

CEOs committed to staying on top of this ever-evolving threat must break down the silos that exist in the organization in order to assess the full dimensions of the risks across the enterprise and address these exposures holistically. The consequences of not doing so could cost them the trust of their shareholders and customers and even their jobs.

Members of the C-suite often aren't speaking the same language around cyber risk, and reporting lines are reinforcing silos. For instance, the general counsel thinks about the issue in terms of compliance with information security regulations such as the European Union's General Data Protection Regulation. The chief information security officer (CISO) or chief information officer (CIO) reports the technical vulnerabilities that his or her team has successfully remediated. The chief risk officer (CRO) looks at the problem in terms of risk transfer and cyber insurance purchased. And the chief financial officer is looking at the potential financial impact.

This lack of communication and coordination across functions makes it very difficult to assess the impact of cyber risk on the business as a whole or create any common metrics for doing so. It also makes it difficult to prioritize the risks that need to be dealt with most urgently while also making it more challenging to appropriately direct efforts and resources.

There are several steps that CEOs should take to create a common language around cybersecurity in their organizations.

First, CEOs should bring together the different members of the C-suite so that all stakeholders are communicating and working in partnership to create a realistic and integrated picture of the business's exposure. This includes: identifying critical data and assets that could be at risk; assessing technical vulnerabilities; understanding the threat landscape; appreciating the potential regulatory and compliance consequences of cyberattacks; quantifying the financial implications of attacks (such as business-interruption costs, lawsuits, remediation costs, loss of enterprise value, and damage to brand and reputation); and gaining a more accurate picture of the impact on shareholder value.

The second step is to create a culture that encourages employees to speak openly about cyber-risk exposure without fear of negative repercussions. It's rare that a CEO motivates key members of the C-suite—especially the CISO or CRO—to report the seriousness of a company's exposures as they evolve. Because cyber risk is dynamic, CEOs must create an environment where there are continual conversations about the impact on security of new events—such as the introduction of new technologies and systems, new cyberthreats, and mergers and acquisitions that involve combining different organizations' information systems and security cultures.

As part of this effort, CEOs should proactively get to know the people outside of the C-suite working in the security trenches. The more CEOs speak with system engineers and technical teams, the more comfortable they will be asking questions about the organization's security. If the CRO and the CISO are reporting only on what's going well, then alarm bells should be ringing.

Third, CEOs should prepare for cyberattacks to ensure everyone knows what to do and can communicate effectively with each other during an incident. There should be a customized incident-response plan that is routinely tested via simulated attacks, which can also test a company's vulnerabilities. A plan can help minimize business disruption, reduce the time attackers have to steal critical data or money, and reduce the amount of damage.

An incident-response plan should include four phases: preparation; detection and analysis; containment, eradication, and recovery; and post-incident.

The preparation phase is the most important since creating a response plan during an incident will not work. Planning helps all stakeholders understand their role and responsibilities, from what constitutes a security incident to who initiates the plan. It also helps leadership communicate with confidence during a real incident both internally to senior executives and members of the board and externally to customers, outside counsel, insurance companies, regulators, and law enforcement.

In the detection-and-analysis phase, the security team determines the scope of the incident and collects the data necessary for analysis. The third phase is about containment: stopping the attack from spreading by removing any infection from the system and fixing any vulnerabilities uncovered. The post-incident phase is a review of what went well, what went wrong, and what can be done better next time.

Outside cybersecurity experts can help develop the plan. But even if an outside firm is not involved, CEOs should at least consider having one test the plan's effectiveness and, crucially, ensure that an external firm is engaged on an incident-response retainer ahead of an incident. You don't want to be struggling to negotiate the fine print of contract terms during an attack.

Finally, companies should create an internal function, led by a chief vulnerability officer, to conduct regular audits of the company's preparedness. This unit, which should report directly to the CEO, should also stage simulated attacks on the business—in addition to those carried out by the CISO or CIO. It should leverage external cyber experts with up-to-date perspectives on the latest cybersecurity methods, threats, and trends to provide unbiased perspectives and help challenge management decisions.

A CEO should enlist all functions in the effort to establish common metrics to assess cyber risks so everyone is speaking the same language and should build a culture of security through open dialogue, planning, and testing. Then, when he or she asks questions—such as "What are our greatest risks?" "What are our critical assets?" "Who has access to them?" "What is our current information security policy?" "What is our incident response plan?" "When was it last tested?"—the answers will yield a more accurate picture.

Only when a CEO understands the true exposure of the business to cyber risks can he or she prioritize the allocation of resources to manage them.

TAKEAWAYS

CEOs need to lead the adoption of a common language around cybersecurity to make it easier to assess, prioritize, and address risks:

- ✓ Assemble all the members of the C-suite and partner to map a realistic and integrated picture of exposure risks.

- ✓ Create an open culture where employees can comfortably engage in continual conversations about topics such as cyber risk exposure, new technologies and systems, and the impact of a merger and acquisition on the affected organizations' information systems and security cultures.

✓ Prepare all employees for cyberattacks by creating and communicating a response plan and routinely testing it with simulated attacks.

✓ Conduct regular audits of the company's preparedness.

Adapted from content posted on hbr.org, November 17, 2017 (product #H040UR).

6

THE BEST CYBERSECURITY INVESTMENT YOU CAN MAKE IS BETTER TRAINING

by Dante Disparte and Chris Furlow

As the scale and complexity of the cyberthreat landscape is revealed, so too is the general lack of cybersecurity readiness in organizations, even those that spend hundreds of millions of dollars on state-of-the-art technology. Investors who have flooded the cybersecurity market in search of the next software "unicorn" have yet to realize that when it comes to a risk as complex as this one, there is no panacea—certainly not one that depends on technology alone.

Spending millions on security technology can certainly make an executive *feel* safe. But the major sources of cyberthreats aren't technological. They're found in the human brain, in the form of curiosity, ignorance, apathy, and hubris. These human forms of malware can be present in any organization and are every bit as dangerous as threats delivered through malicious code.

With any cyberthreat, the first and last line of defense is prepared leaders and employees, whether they are inside an organization or part of an interconnected supply chain.

And yet organizational leadership all too often demonstrates outright technology turpitude. An unprepared, lethargic leadership only amplifies the consequences of a security breach. The scale of the Yahoo breach disclosed in 2016, combined with the fumbling response, cost the company and its shareholders $350 million in its merger with Verizon and nearly scuttled the entire deal.

To prepare for and prevent the cyberattacks of the future, firms need to balance technological deterrents and tripwires with agile, human-centered defenses. These vigorous, people-centric efforts must go beyond the oft-discussed "tone at the top"—they must include a proactive leadership approach with faster, sharper decision making. As cyberthreats grow exponentially, comprehensive risk management is now a board-level priority. Indeed, the iconic investor Warren Buffett highlighted cyber risk as one of the gravest concerns facing humanity during Berkshire Hathaway's annual meeting.

Firms must recognize and react to three uncomfortable truths. First, cyber risk evolves according to Moore's Law. That's a major reason that technology solutions alone can never keep pace with dynamic cyberthreats. Second, as with all threat management, defense is a much harder role to play than offense. The offensive players only need to win once to wreak incalculable havoc on an enterprise. Third, and worst yet, attackers have patience and latency (since most attacks go undetected) on their side. Firms can be lulled into a dangerous state of complacency by their defensive technologies, firewalls, and assurances of perfect cyber hygiene.

The danger is in thinking that these risks can be perfectly "managed" through some sort of comprehensive defense system. It's better to assume your defenses will be breached and to train your people in what to do when that happens. Instead of "risk management," we propose thinking of it as "risk agility." The agile enterprise equips *all* organizational layers with decision guideposts and boundaries to set thresholds of risk tolerance. All employees should not only understand what is expected of them regarding company policy and online behavior but also be trained to recognize nefarious or suspicious activity.

The key attribute, particularly when it relates to cyber risk, is the concept of *sense something, do something*, which makes all people in an organization a part of a "neural safety network." For example, the defense against the SWIFT banking hack, in which some $81 million was stolen, was launched by an alert banking clerk in Germany who recognized a misspelling.

When we say all employees have to be risk agile, we mean *all*. C-level executives, board directors, shareholders, and other senior leaders must not only invest in training for their firm's own employees but also consider how to evaluate and inform the outsiders upon whom their businesses rely—contractors, consultants, and vendors in their supply chains. Such third parties with access to company networks have enabled high-profile breaches, including Target and Home Depot, among others.

A skeptical executive could push back on this idea— *won't that cost a lot?* The fact is, cybersecurity training is vastly undercapitalized, and the lack of investment in quality cyber education programs is manifest in the sheer volume of breaches that continue to be rooted in human failure. Worse, the volume of breaches is woefully underreported—even when they are identified early because firms are reluctant to amplify reputation risk. In a 2016 survey conducted by CSO magazine and the CERT Division of the Software Engineering Institute of Carnegie Mellon University, respondents reported that insiders were the source of "50% of incidents where private or sensitive information was unintentionally exposed." Insider threats can include malicious activities but also mistakes by employees, such as falling for a phishing scam.

In short, there will be some investment required in enhancing personnel readiness. But it can be cost effective over time, particularly when compared to implementing cutting-edge cybersecurity technology that may become obsolete. To be clear, technology is a critical piece of the cybersecurity puzzle, but just as with a car containing all the latest safety technology, the best defense remains a well-trained driver.

Moreover, businesses slow to adopt stronger security measures may find themselves pushed into it by regulators. The latest regulations promulgated by the New York State Department of Financial Services, for example, require that covered businesses "provide regular cybersecurity awareness training for all personnel." This is just the tip of the iceberg of what is likely to come from other states and government agencies around the world, which are increasingly harmonizing their view of a "carrots and sticks" approach to cybersecurity compliance.

Artificial intelligence, machine learning, and self-teaching algorithms may represent the latest trends in hot IT investments, but technology exists for and is utilized by *people*. Corporate leaders would be wise to understand that the future of cybersecurity lies not in a single-pronged approach or miracle tool but in solutions that recognize the importance of layering human readiness on top of technological defenses.

TAKEAWAYS

Investing a lot of money and resources in security technology can make companies *feel* safe, but the major threats to an organization's cybersecurity aren't technological—they're human shortcomings:

✓ Technology solutions alone will never be able to keep pace with dynamic cyberthreats.

✓ Defense is harder to play than offense; attackers have patience and latency on their side and only need to win once to wreak havoc on an organization.

✓ Assume your company will endure breaches and train *all* employees (from executives to contractors) in how to recognize suspicious activity and what to do when a breach occurs.

Adapted from content posted on hbr.org, May 16, 2017 (product #H03NVF).

7

BETTER CYBERSECURITY STARTS WITH FIXING YOUR EMPLOYEES' BAD HABITS

by Alex Blau

ybercrime is here to stay, and it's costing American firms a lot of money. The average annualized cost of cybercrime for global companies has increased nearly 62% since 2013, from $7.2 million to $11.7 million.[1] And these are just the average direct costs. Target, which experienced a massive data breach in 2013, reported that the total cost of the breach exceeded $200 million.[2] Given these costs, what can companies do?

Governments and industry are doing what seems like the obvious thing to do—spending billions of dollars to develop and implement new technologies designed to stop the bad guys before they can get through the front door. Yet, even though we have some of the best and brightest minds on the case, there are still major limitations to what we can do with silicon and code. Despite our predilection for using technology to solve what appear to be technological problems, one lament that echoes in information security circles is that we're not doing enough to deal with cybersecurity's biggest, most persistent threat—human behavior.

In 2014, IBM reported that "over 95% of all [security] incidents investigated recognize 'human error' as a contributing factor."[3] In fact, the string of malware attacks with cyberpunk appellations such as "Wanna-Cry," "Petya," and "Mirai," as well as the apparent state-sponsored attacks on Equifax and the American electoral system, all started because of poor decisions and actions from end users. If it wasn't an engineer inadvertently building a vulnerability into a piece of software, it was an end user clicking on a bad link, falling for a phishing attack, using a weak password, or neglecting to install a security update in a timely manner. Attackers didn't need to break down a wall of ones and zeros or sabotage a piece of sophisticated hardware; instead they simply needed to take advantage of predictably poor user behavior.

When companies focus their attention on solving what they think are technology problems with technology solutions, they'll neglect to identify simple interventions that can help reduce the incidence of bad behaviors and promote good ones. And yes, while some technology investments have sought to prevent these behaviors in the first place by offloading human decisions onto artificial intelligence and machine learning systems, these innovations still have some way to go. As the security robot that fell into a mall fountain reminds us, AI and related innovations are not yet fully developed technologies. For example, how many times has your spam filter missed a phishing email? In the absence of fail-proof AI, human judgment is still needed to fill the gap between the capabilities of our security technologies and our security needs. But if human judgment isn't perfect, and technology isn't enough, what can companies do to reduce behavioral risks?

One major insight from the fields of behavioral economics and psychology is that our behavioral biases are quite predictable. For instance, security professionals have said time and again that keeping software up-to-date, and installing security patches as soon as possible, is one of the best methods of protecting information security systems from attacks. However, even though installing updates is a relative no-brainer, many users and even IT administrators procrastinate on this critical step. Why? Part of the problem is that update prompts and patches often come at the wrong time—when the person responsible for installing the update is preoccupied with some other, presently pressing issue. Additionally, when it comes to updating our personal computers and devices, we're often provided with an easy "out" in the form of a "remind me later" option. Because of this small contextual detail, users are much more likely to defer on the update, no matter how critical. How many times have you clicked on the "remind me tomorrow" option before finally committing to the update?

At ideas42, my behavioral science research and design firm, we've been documenting the various contexts that lead users and administrators to decide (and act) in less-than-optimal ways, placing themselves and their companies at greater risk for a cyberattack. Through this lens, we've generated a number of insights about why people set bad passwords, neglect to install updates, click on malicious links, and fall for phishing emails. We've also outlined what organizations and administrators can do to improve their users' behavior. (To learn more, check out our research-based true-crime novella, *Deep Thought: A Cybersecurity Story*).

Set strong defaults

One of the most influential insights from the behavioral sciences is that whatever is in the "default" position generally sticks. This insight has been used to great effect in the domains of retirement savings and organ donation, where a shift from an "opt-in" to an "opt-out" default has significantly increased participation rates. Similar logic could be applied to the choice context around enterprise user security. Instead of having your employees opt in to specific security actions such as installing and using a VPN, turning on two-factor authentication, enabling full-disc encryption, or authorizing auto-update features, employers could take the time to set up computers and systems that employees use to have these features turned on by default. Doing so could lead to higher rates of compliance than trusting your employees to do it for themselves.

Use calendar commitments to nudge system updating

Sometimes enabling auto-updates for system software isn't possible, leaving the choice of whether to update in the hands of employees. However, when facing the prospect of halting workflow to update some software, employees may decide to defer the action until some ambiguous "better time." The problem is that if we remain *present biased*, focused on the current task at hand, that "better time" may never come along. One way researchers have been able to get around this present-bias problem is to get users to make concrete commitments about when they'll follow through—the more specific the better. In the context of software updates, employers could help facilitate employees in making a concrete commitment to update. For instance, when an update is released, an administrator could send an email instructing employees to block off a time on their calendar to complete the update. The simple act of getting employees to pre-commit can stop the procrastination cycle dead in its tracks.

Compare employees to their peers

People have a tendency to look toward other people, especially those who are similar to them, to learn how to act. This phenomenon, called *social proof,* can have powerful effects on people's behavior, and it is especially influential when the desirable behavior is ambiguous—such as with cyber hygiene. Opower, a customer engagement platform for utility providers, has used this insight to great effect. The company sends a small infographic along with households' utility bills showing how much energy the household is consuming relative to the average household in their neighborhood, as well as the most efficient ones. This small indication of what other households are doing reduces average energy consumption by 2% per household, which, at scale, is a huge change.[4]

What this and similar interventions have shown is that people don't actually need to *see* others exhibit a specific behavior; they can instead be told what others do. In an enterprise setting, administrators can leverage social proof to help employees identify desirable behaviors and motivate them to take them on. For instance, employers could poll employees about various behaviors and safeguards they use online and assign a score based on those behaviors. They could then produce reports for each individual comparing them to the average employee, as well as the most diligent employees, and provide them with actionable steps they can take to improve their score. This simple social proof intervention could lead to greater compliance across an organization.

Turn awareness training into a constant feedback system

One major insight from behavioral science is that if you provide someone training, you might increase people's knowledge, but you aren't likely to change their behaviors. Often awareness training happens something like this: Once a year, employees get into a room for an hour or two and get lectured at by a professional awareness trainer, only to go back to their workstations and ignore most of what they were taught. There are many reasons why this might happen: People have limited attention and can't absorb all the information they just learned; they may not have a concrete sense of how to make what they learned actionable and so don't change their behavior; they may be overconfident that none of the risks they learned about apply to them in particular ("it will never happen to me!"); and the list goes on.

One way that enterprises may improve the efficacy of awareness training is to make it an ongoing process, building in feedback so that employees learn about when they mess up and what they can do to avoid that error in the future. For instance, to make your workforce more resilient to phishing attacks, you might choose to employ software like Phishme, which sends out fake phishing emails to employees on a regular basis, and provides remediation when users fall for the attack. Similar processes could be put in place to help employees avoid bad links, remember to update their software, and take on other beneficial behaviors such as using two-factor authentication, turning on their VPN when accessing an insecure network, and utilizing more secure passwords.

If we keep trying to use technology to solve what are in reality human problems, we'll continue to remain vulnerable to attacks. However, if we take an approach that looks at the context in which human beings are liable to make mistakes, we will be more likely to find sustainable solutions that will keep ourselves, and our enterprises, safe from the bad guys.

TAKEAWAYS

When companies focus only on solving what they perceive to be technology problems with technology solutions, attackers can take advantage of the predictable behavioral human biases that increase risk:

✓ Since default positions generally stick, shift to "opt-out" to increase participation rates in security measures such as installing and using a VPN or enabling a two-factor authentication.

✓ Overcome present bias—where people are focused on the task at hand—and get users to create concrete commitments about when they'll install a software update by blocking off time on their calendar to do so.

✓ Take advantage of people's tendency to behave how those around them behave by sharing data about what their colleagues are doing—like those energy usage infographics utility companies distribute that compare your usage with your neighbors'. Poll employees about various behaviors and safeguards they use when they're online and share those results along with actionable steps people can take to improve their score.

✓ Make awareness training an ongoing process, with built-in feedback, to help employees learn about where they erred and what they can do to avoid similar mistakes in the future.

NOTES

1. Accenture and Ponemon Institute, "2017 Cost of Cyber Crime Study," https://www.accenture.com/us-en/insight-cost-of-cybercrime-2017.

2. Robert Hackett, "How Much Do Data Breaches Cost Big Companies? Shockingly Little," *Fortune*, March 27, 2015, http://fortune.com/2015/03/27/how-much-do-data-breaches-actually-cost-big-companies-shockingly-little/.

3. IBM, "IBM Security Services 2014 Cyber Security Intelligence Index," https://media.scmagazine.com/documents/82/ibm_cyber_security_intelligenc_20450.pdf.

4. Hunt Allcott and Todd Rogers, "Opower: Evaluating the Impact of Home Energy Reports on Energy Conservation in the United States," J-PAL, https://www.povertyactionlab.org/evaluation /opower-evaluating-impact-home-energy-reports-energy -conservation-united-states.

Adapted from content posted on hbr.org, December 11, 2017 (product H0428V).

8

THE KEY TO BETTER CYBERSECURITY

Keep Employee Rules Simple

by Maarten Van Horenbeeck

I t's a common adage that employees are the weak link in corporate cybersecurity. But I believe they are also the best defense, *if* they are given policies that are easy to follow and not too numerous and complex. Employee security training and best practices need to be user friendly and simple to be effective.

Cyberattackers don't need to have advanced hacking skills to break into corporate networks; they just need to know how to trick people into opening attachments and clicking on links. Phishing attacks are the cause of 90% of all data breaches and security incidents, according to the latest Verizon Data Breach Investigations Report.[1] Clearly, employees are the main gateway into the organization for attackers. As a result, they are also the first line of defense. The Verizon report found that employee notifications are the most common way organizations discover cyberattacks. So arming these "sentry" employees with information they need to identify attacks is a critical part of a company's overall security program—and yet most companies fail at this.

Security Shortcuts

One of the big reasons security rules often don't work is because they are so complex that they drive people to take shortcuts that defeat their purpose. For example, password policies are so complicated and inconvenient that most employees just ignore them. Employees are told to change passwords frequently, but researchers have found that when people are required to come up with new passwords every three months they tend to do things like merely capitalizing the first letter or adding a number on the end to save time.[2] This makes passwords increasingly easier to crack. Being creative gets exhausting when you have to do it repeatedly, yet most companies force this requirement on employees for the sake of security.

Another example of a self-defeating security policy is requiring long and complex passwords. We're constantly being told to come up with complicated passwords, ideally strings of passphrases that incorporate numerals, uppercase letters, and symbols. When faced with this task, many employees will simply ignore the policy or create a long password that can't easily be remembered—so they write it on a Post-it note attached to the monitor. Again, these are practices that provide a false sense of security for the organization.

These historical password guidelines are finally being challenged now that they have proven to be ineffective for most organizations. The U.S. National Institute of Standards and Technology (NIST) recently changed its guidelines to reflect this reality, and now recommends getting rid of rules that complicate password practices for end users, such as requiring frequent password resets.[3] They recommend allowing the use of password managers and allowing people to paste passwords into fields. They also recommend multi-factor authentication, such as codes sent to smartphones and key fobs.

Teachable Moments

Another reason internal cybersecurity practices don't work is that employees are so overwhelmed with guidance and information about things they should and shouldn't do that they can't digest it all. They are shuttled into mandatory half-day security training sessions, at which they often spend time staring at their phones or pretending to pay attention. It's too much information to expect someone to absorb and remember, but for IT serves a purpose: enabling admins to report back to their department heads that they have trained employees on security best practices. It's a compliance action that isn't effective and wastes employee time.

I advise IT admins to instead do what hackers do to be effective—customize their work as much as possible. For instance, the most dangerous phishing emails—spear-phishing attacks that are targeted at high-value employees—work because they are customized to fool exactly the person they are sent to. Requests for tax information and fake wire transfer requests look like they are sent from the CEO or CFO to someone in the finance department using the appropriate language. People fall for them because attackers have paid attention to detail. IT departments should follow the same playbook and use customized training and guidance rather than general and comprehensive trainings for all employees. I refer to this technique as "teachable moments" because it provides targeted information to specific individuals in a way and time they are most likely to be receptive to and able to learn from.

Most internal security tests are too broad and unfocused. For example, IT departments tend to do phishing tests by sending out the same fake email to all employees. I don't think these phishing tests are appropriate for all organizations. "Testing your users" requires a lot of framing and engagement to ensure that it doesn't make employees feel untrusted, and thus reduce the trust relationship they have with their security team.

The same principle holds true for third-party sharing and collaboration services, such as Slack and Dropbox. When we try to block these common tools, often the user will find and use a different one that IT failed to block. If IT instead identifies when employees use the service, and provides targeted guidance on how to use it securely, or offers a corporate subscription with security education, they can make a far bigger impact.

A Culture of Openness

An often-overlooked aspect of employee security practices is the relationship between the employee and the
IT department and security team. In most organizations,
employees view the security team as the traffic cops of
the enterprise who are constantly telling them they can't
do something they want to do, like download an external software program. Employees also complain about
delayed IT responses to help-desk tickets, and an adver-
sarial relationship tends to develop. This situation needs
to change if organizations want to improve the security
practices of employees. The security and IT teams need
to be seen as trusted and helpful advisers to employees,
instead of as regulators.

The best way to change this dynamic is to increase the
opportunities for interaction between employees and IT.
This can be in the form of office hours, when employees
can seek help and information for IT and security issues
and not be treated as an annoyance. And IT can be more
proactive about getting to know employees and finding
out what they are experiencing by mingling more among
employees, instead of just showing up when someone requests something.

The single most important thing companies can do
is improve the relationship between IT and employees,

who are the closest to the data and devices, and thus in the best position to discover and report security anomalies and incidents. Getting to know the employees, what their roles are, and how they work with technology, will increase the chance that they will report security issues and be more conscientious in their security practices. It also can help provide IT the information they need to tailor their security education and testing efforts to individuals. It will take collaboration like this within the organization to really change peoples' habits and make a difference in keeping organizations safe.

TAKEAWAYS

Employees are the weakest link in cybersecurity. But they can become your company's best defense if the policies they're given are easy to follow and not too numerous or complicated:

✓ Security rules, such as impossibly complex password requirements, are often so onerous that people take shortcuts that defeat their purpose. Ease this burden by allowing password managers or using multi-factor authentication.

✓ Swap mandatory day-long training sessions for customized training and guidance.

✓ The IT department are often seen as "regulators" by the rest of your company. Change this dynamic by making IT trusted and helpful advisers to your other employees by increasing opportunities for interaction through casual office hours or informal gatherings.

NOTES

1. Verizon, "2017 Data Breach Investigations Report," https://enterprise.verizon.com/resources/reports/2017_dbir.pdf.

2. Yinqian Zhang, Fabian Monrose, and Michael K. Reiter, "The Security of Modern Password Expiration: An Algorithmic Framework and Empirical Analysis," in *Proceedings of the 17th ACM Conference on Computer and Communications Security*, October 4, 2010, https://www.cs.unc.edu/~reiter/papers/2010/CCS.pdf.

3. Paul A. Grassi, Michael E. Garcia, and James L. Fenton, "Digital Identity Guidelines," National Institute of Standards and Technology, June 2017, https://pages.nist.gov/800-63-3/sp800-63-3.html.

Adapted from content posted on hbr.org, November 21, 2017 (product #H04153).

9

THE AVOIDABLE MISTAKES EXECUTIVES CONTINUE TO MAKE AFTER A DATA BREACH

by Bill Bourdon

The past few years have taught us that companies *will* be breached and consumer data *will* be stolen. Still, top executives continue to stumble in the way they respond to an attack, magnifying and extending the damage both to their reputation and their customers.

In analyzing the top breaches over the past few years, it is clear that executives make a set of common mistakes, which is surprising given that so many companies, often led by otherwise effective leaders, fail to learn from the botched responses and mishandled situations of the companies that were breached before them.

Here are the missteps executives make time and again, and advice for avoiding these pitfalls:

Foot Dragging

The longer companies wait to notify their customers, the greater the chance criminals will be able to use stolen data. While Equifax got blasted for taking nearly six weeks to disclose its breach, at least it didn't wait until the stolen data was being sold on the dark web to go public with the news. Target didn't comment on their breach until nearly a week *after* it was reported by security blogger Brian Krebs. More recently, it came to light that the SEC waited a full year before disclosing information about its breach.

Executives today must operate under the assumption that they will experience a cyber incident that will require them to notify their customers, investors, and regulators. The immediate emotional response may be to wait until all the details are available and carefully messaged, but it is negligent to withhold information that could help people keep their data and finances safe. The best way to assure executives and their communications teams respond to breaches quickly is to have a well-oiled incident response plan in place. It appears Whole Foods had a plan in place as the company reported its 2017 breach five days after detection.

A federal breach notification law mandating quicker response times would also better serve citizens who are now at the mercy of a patchwork of state laws that have limits ranging from 15 days to 90 days, if they have limits at all. By contrast, an EU law that took effect in 2018 as part of the General Data Protection Regulation (GDPR) gives companies 72 hours.

Poor Customer Service

In 2016, Yahoo CEO Marissa Mayer failed to take a basic step that could have quickly protected customers whose accounts were exposed in a breach that occurred two years earlier: Automatically reset all user passwords. This would have immediately blocked criminals from getting into those accounts, but Mayer reportedly declined to do it because it would have forced all users to create new passwords, and she was worried that they would be annoyed and drop Yahoo.

After its breach, Equifax originally offered customers free credit reporting for one year if they waived their rights to sue. In addition, Equifax tried to profit from its mistake by charging people who wanted to freeze their reports as an added layer of protection. The company soon dropped this condition, extended free credit reporting for life, and waived the credit freeze fees, but by that time the reputational damage had been done.

The top priority for Yahoo should have been to do whatever it could to immediately protect customers. Equifax should have offered free, condition-free monitoring to help consumers stay safe. Top corporate officers need to make sure their gestures of goodwill align with the severity of the breach, even if they are expensive to implement.

Not Being Transparent

Being open in the aftermath of a breach is the thing executives are in a position to control—but more often than not, they evade the truth. Transparency is a cornerstone to rebuilding trust in the brand.

In spite of its many other breach-response blunders, Equifax was fairly diligent in keeping the public updated on information related to its breach. In addition to distributing a press release and posting a video to their site (about five weeks after they discovered the breach), Equifax created a dedicated website for breach-related news that was updated five times in the week following the press release and video posting. However, on multiple occasions, the company's official Twitter account directed customers to a fake phishing site. The official site had multiple technical difficulties, and when it was available, the site required people to verify their identity with the last six digits of their social security numbers—providing precisely the kind of personal information that was hacked in the first place.

Sony handled its PlayStation Network (PSN) breach even worse. After discovering the network intrusion, Sony shut it down but didn't say anything about being breached until two days later. Details about the incident trickled out haphazardly over the following weeks, and the advice offered by Sony to customers was muddled.

By issuing confusing and incorrect information about a breach, executives prevent customers from taking actions they need to take in order to protect themselves. A lack of transparency also leads customers to believe executives are withholding information—even if they aren't.

It's okay to say "we don't know at this time." Being honest and authentic, and providing clear and frequent updates, will earn trust from customers who just want to be leveled with.

Failing to Accept Accountability

A massive breach is not an individual error or a technology failure—it's an organizational breakdown that is the responsibility of the top executive. It might not be a surprise that top executives don't typically see it that way. A study from risk-management firm Stroz Friedberg found that just 45% of senior leaders believe they are responsible for protecting their companies against cyberattacks.

It took 11 days after the Sony breach for any executives to apologize for the breach and 26 days for Sony chairman Howard Stringer to do so publicly. Equifax CEO Richard Smith initially showed humility and accountability in the immediate aftermath of the company's breach, saying in a video: "I deeply regret this incident and I apologize to every affected consumer and all of our partners." But after he was forced to resign, in his testimony before a U.S. House committee, Smith blamed an employee for failing to take basic security measures.

Until more top executives begin to hold themselves accountable for cyber incidents, and learn from the mistakes that others have made before them, we will continue to see breaches and poor leadership in the responses to these attacks.

TAKEAWAYS

When executives flub their response to a breach, they magnify and extend the damage to their customers, their organization—and to their own reputation:

✓ Leaders often make the same set of mistakes after an attack: They wait too long to notify customers, they deliver subpar service to customers once they do communicate the breach, they issue confusing and incorrect information about the attack, and they fail to accept accountability.

✓ Executives should expect to experience a breach and have an incident response plan in place before they need it.

✓ Customers should be a primary focus of care and leaders should take proactive measures to protect them through steps such as automatically resetting user passwords or offering free credit reporting.

✓ Rebuild trust in your brand by sharing clear and regular updates with customers.

✓ Recognize that a breach is not a technological failure; own that it's an organizational breakdown that is your responsibility as the top executive.

Adapted from content posted on hbr.org, November 20, 2017 (product #H04127).

ACTIVE DEFENSE
AND "HACKING BACK"

A Primer

by Scott Berinato

Earlier in this book, Idaho National Lab's Andy Bochman put forth a provocative idea: that no amount of spending on technology defenses can secure your critical systems or help you keep pace with hackers. To protect your most valuable information, he argues, you need to move beyond so-called cyber hygiene, the necessary but insufficient deployment of security software and network-monitoring processes.

Bochman lays out a framework that requires switching your focus from the benefits of efficiency to the costs. Ideas that were once anathema—unplug some systems from the internet, de-automate in some places, insert trusted humans back into the process—are now the smart play.

But they're not the only play. Another that's gaining attention is "active defense." That might sound like Orwellian doublespeak, but it's a real strategy. It involves going beyond passive monitoring and taking proactive measures to deal with the constant attacks on your network.

There's just one problem: As active defense tactics gain popularity, the term's definition and tenets have become a muddy mess. Most notably, active defense has been conflated with "hacking back"—attacking your attackers. The approaches are not synonymous; there are important differences with respect to ethics, legality, and effectiveness.

Active defense has a place in every company's critical infrastructure-protection scheme. But to effectively deploy it, you need a proper understanding of what it is—and that's tougher to come by than you might expect.

We enlisted two of the foremost experts on the topic to help us proffer an authoritative definition of active defense and provide a fundamental understanding of how to deploy it.

Dorothy Denning was an inaugural inductee into the National Cyber Security Hall of Fame. A fellow of the Association for Computing Machinery and a professor at the Naval Postgraduate School, she has written several books on cybersecurity, including *Information Warfare and Security*. She also coauthored a landmark paper on active defense, which states, "When properly understood, [active defense] is neither offensive nor necessarily dangerous."

Robert M. Lee is a cofounder of Dragos, an industrial security firm. He conducted cyber operations for the NSA and U.S. Cyber Command from 2011 to 2015. In October 2017 his firm identified the first known malware written specifically to target industrial safety systems— in other words, its sole purpose was to damage or destroy systems meant to protect people. (The malware had been deployed that August against a petrochemical plant in Saudi Arabia, but the attack failed.) When asked about active defense, Lee sighs and asks flatly, "How are you defining it?" You can tell he's had this conversation before. The number of people co-opting the term seems to have wearied him, and he's happy to help bring clarity to the idea.

The following FAQ primer draws on interviews with Denning and Lee.

What exactly is active defense, also known as active cyber defense?

It depends on whom you ask. The term has almost as many definitions as it does citations. NATO defines active defense this way: "A proactive measure for detecting or obtaining information as to a cyber intrusion, cyberattack, or impending cyber operation or for determining the origin of an operation that involves launching a preemptive, preventive, or cyber counter-operation against the source."

A solid working definition can be found in Denning's paper with Bradley J. Strawser, "Active Cyber Defense: Applying Air Defense to the Cyber Domain": "*Active cyber defense* is a direct defensive action taken to destroy, nullify, or reduce the effectiveness of cyber threats against friendly forces and assets."

That sounds like offense, but Lee and Denning note that it describes a strictly defensive action—one taken in reaction to a detected infiltration. Lee argues that there's a border distinction: Active defense happens when someone crosses into your space, be it over a political boundary or a network boundary. But Denning says that's probably too simple, and below we'll see a case in which the line is blurred. Lee says, "Most experts understand this, but it's important to point out, especially for a general audience. You are prepared to actively deal with malicious actors who have crossed into your space. Sending missiles into someone else's space is offense. Monitoring for missiles coming at you is passive defense. Shooting them down when they cross into your airspace is active defense."

Can you give some other examples?

Denning says, "One example of active cyber defense is a system that monitors for intrusions, detects one, and responds by blocking further network connections from the source and alerting the system administrator. Another example is taking steps to identify and shut down a botnet used to conduct distributed denial-of-service (DDoS) attacks." It's the verbs "responds" and "shut down" that make these instances of active defense. An example of passive defense, in contrast, is an encryption system that renders communications or stored data useless to spies and thieves.

Is active defense only an information security concept?

Not at all. Some argue that it dates back to *The Art of War*, in which Sun Tzu wrote, "Security against defeat implies defensive tactics; ability to defeat the enemy means taking the offensive." Centuries later Mao Zedong said, "The only real defense is active defense," equating it to the destruction of an enemy's ability to attack—much as aggressive tactics in active cyber defense aim to do. The term was applied in the Cold War and, as Denning and Strawser's paper makes clear, is a core concept in air missile defense. Tactics are tactics; all that changes is where they're employed.

That seems pretty straightforward. So why the uncertainty around the definition?

As noted earlier, hacking back—also not a new term—has confused matters. Properly used, it refers to efforts to attack your attackers *on their turf.* But because people often conflate it with active defense, difficult and sometimes frustrating disputes over the merits of active defense have ensued. One research paper went so far as to equate the two terms, starting its definition, "Hack back—sometimes termed 'active defense' . . ."

The confusion multiplied in October 2017, when Representatives Tom Graves (R-GA) and Kyrsten Sinema (D-AZ) introduced the Active Cyber Defense Certainty (ACDC) bill, which would allow companies to gain unauthorized access to computers in some situations in order to disrupt attacks. The lawmakers called this active defense. The media called it the "hack back bill." What it would and would not allow became the subject of hot debate. The idea that companies could go into other people's infected computers wasn't welcomed. Some savaged the bill. The technology blog network Engadget called it "smarmy and conceited" and observed, "When you try to make laws about hacking based on a child's concept of 'getting someone back,' you're getting very far and away from making yourself secure. It's like trying to make gang warfare productive." The bill went through two iterations and is currently stalled, as of the time this book went to press.

But is hacking back part of active defense?

Probably not. Lee says unequivocally, "Hacking back is absolutely not active defense. It's probably illegal, and it's probably not effective. We don't have evidence that attacking attackers works." Denning has a somewhat different take. "Hacking back is just one form of active defense," she says. "It might be used to gather intelligence about the source of an intrusion to determine attribution or what data might have been stolen. If the attacker is identified, law enforcement might bring charges. If stolen data is found on the intruder's system, it might be deleted. Hacking back might also involve neutralizing or shutting down an attacking system so that it cannot cause further damage."

But Lee and Denning are defining the term differently. And Denning's version refers to actions undertaken with proper authority by government entities. When it comes to hacking back on the part of businesses, the two experts are in total agreement: Don't do it. Denning says, "Companies should not hack back. The Department of Justice has advised victims of cyberattacks to refrain from any 'attempt to access, damage, or impair another system that may appear to be involved in the intrusion or attack.' The advice contends that 'doing so is likely illegal, under U.S. and some foreign laws, and could result in civil and/or criminal liability.'"

What's an example of an aggressive form of active defense that some might consider hacking back?

Denning says,

> One of my favorite examples of active defense led to the exposure of a Russian hacker who had gotten malicious code onto government computers in the country of Georgia. The malware searched for documents using keywords such as "USA" and "NATO,"

which it then uploaded to a drop server used by the hacker. The Georgian government responded by planting spyware in a file named "Georgian-NATO Agreement" on one of its compromised machines. The hacker's malware dutifully found and uploaded the file to the drop server, which the hacker then downloaded to his own machine. The spyware turned on the hacker's webcam and sent incriminating files along with a snapshot of his face back to the Georgian government.

Is that hacking back? I don't think so. It was really through the hacker's own code and actions that he ended up with spyware on his computer.

Note that the actions were taken by a government and occurred within its "borders"; Georgia put the spyware on its own computer. It did not traverse a network to hit another system. It was the hacker's action of illegally taking the file that triggered the surveillance.

If it's probably illegal and ineffective, why is hacking back getting so much press?

Companies are weary. "They are under constant attack and working so hard and spending so much just to keep up, and they *can't* keep up," Lee says. "This is a moment when we're looking for new ideas. That's why Bochman's concept of unplugging systems and not always going right to the most efficient solution is starting to be heard. Hacking back feels like another way to turn the tide. Cybersecurity loves a silver bullet, and this feels like one. CEOs are probably thinking, 'Nothing else has worked; let's fight.'" Lee has heard many business leaders express these sentiments, especially if their companies have suffered damaging attacks. "This is an emotional issue," he says. "You feel violated, and you want to do something about it."

In a paper titled "Ethics of Hacking Back," Cal Poly's Patrick Lin captures the sense of utter vulnerability that could lead some to desire vigilante justice:

> In cybersecurity, there's a certain sense of helplessness—you are mostly on your own. You are often the first and last line of defense for your information and communications technologies; there is no equivalent of state-protected borders, neighborhood police patrols, and other public protections in cyberspace.
>
> For instance, if your computer were hit by "ransomware"—malware that locks up your system until you pay a fee to extortionists—law enforcement would likely be unable to help you. The U.S. Federal Bureau of Investigation (FBI) offers this

guidance: "To be honest, we often advise people to just pay the ransom," according to Joseph Bonavolonta, the assistant special agent in charge of the FBI's cyber and counterintelligence program.

Do not expect a digital cavalry to come to your rescue in time. As online life moves at digital speeds, law enforcement and state responses are often too slow to protect, prosecute, or deter cyberattackers. To be sure, some prosecutions are happening but inconsistently and slowly. The major cases that make headlines are conspicuously unresolved, even if authorities confidently say they know who did them.

What are the ethics of hacking back?

For the most part, experts say that hacking back without legal authorization or government cooperation is unethical. And whenever activities leave your boundaries, it's hard to condone them. The targets are too evasive, and the networks are too complex, traversing innocent systems and affecting the people working with them. In addition, Lee points out that government entities might be tracking and dealing with malicious actors, and hacking back could compromise their operations. "Leave it to the pros," he says.

Denning stresses that unintended consequences are not just possible but likely. She says, "The biggest risks come when you start messing with someone else's computers. Many cyberattacks are launched through intermediary machines that were previously compromised by the attacker. Those computers could be anywhere, even in a hospital or power plant. So you don't want to shut them down or cause them to malfunction."

What kind of work is under way with regard to ethics?

According to Denning, researchers began wrestling with these issues as early as 2006. Speaking about a workshop she participated in, she says, "I recall discussions about measures that involved tracing back through a series of compromised machines to find the origin of an attack. Such tracebacks would involve hacking into the compromised machines to get their logs if the owners were not willing or could not be trusted to help out."

A decade later Denning collaborated with Strawser to examine the morality of active defense writ large, using the ethics of air defense and general war doctrine as a guide. They wrote that harm to "non-combatants"—especially and most obviously physical harm—disqualifies an active defense strategy. But they say that "temporary harm to the *property* of non-combatants" is sometimes morally permissible. (It should be noted that Denning is primarily focused on the government use of active cyber defense strategies). Denning cites the takedown of Coreflood—malware that infected millions of computers and was used as a botnet. The Justice Department won approval to seize the botnet by taking over its command-and-control servers. Then, when the bots contacted the servers for instructions, the response was essentially, "Stop operating." In the instance of Coreflood, as in some similar cases, a judge decided that the actions could proceed because they could shut down major malicious code without damaging the infected systems or accessing any information on them.

"The effect was simply to stop the bot code from running. No other functions were affected, and the infected computers continued to operate normally," Denning says. "There was virtually no risk of causing any harm whatsoever, let alone serious harm."

Still, the case may have set a precedent for at least the suggestion of more aggressive measures, such as the ACDC bill. If the government can take control of command-and-control servers, it can, in theory, do more than just tell the bots to shut down. Why not grab some log files at the same time? Or turn on the webcam, as in the Georgian-NATO case? Oversight is needed in all active defense strategies.

How can I deploy an ethical and effective active defense strategy?

If you have or subscribe to services that can thwart DDoS attacks and create logs, you've already started. Denning says that many companies are doing more active defense than they realize. "They might not call it active defense, but what they call it matters less than what they do."

Cooperating with law enforcement and the international network of companies and organizations combating hacking is also part of an active defense strategy. The more companies and agencies that work together, the more likely it is that active defense strategies like the one that took out Coreflood can be executed without harm. Several such operations have taken place without reports of problems.

Denning recommends *A Data-Driven Computer Security Defense: THE Computer Security Defense You Should Be Using,* by Roger A. Grimes. (Full disclosure: Denning wrote the foreword. "But the book really is good!" she says.)

As for more aggressive tactics, like the ones proposed in the ACDC bill, proceed with caution. Work with law enforcement and other government agencies, and understand the risks. Denning says, "It's *all* about risk. Companies need to understand the threats and vulnerabilities and how security incidents will impact their company, customers, and partners. Then they need to select cost-effective security defenses, both passive and active." There are limits, she cautions. "Security is a bottomless pit; you can only do so much. But it's important to do the right things—the things that will make a difference."

TAKEAWAYS

Some companies are going beyond traditional passive monitoring of security and introducing active defense measures to protect their company's mission-critical systems:

✓ There is no consensus among experts of the definition of active defense, but a solid working definition is "active cyber defense is a direct defensive action taken to destroy, nullify, or reduce the effectiveness of cyber threats against friendly forces and assets."

✓ "Hacking back" is another term that defies easy definition, and it is often confused with active defense. Hacking back refers to attempts to attack your attackers on *their* systems, like sending a missile into someone else's space. Active defense is shooting down an attacker's missile when they cross into your airspace.

✓ Despite the lack of consensus on a definition of hacking back, the experts agree that companies should not engage in this practice because it is unethical and possibly illegal.

Adapted from content posted on hbr.org, May 21, 2018 (product #BG1803).

CYBERSECURITY IS PUTTING CUSTOMER TRUST AT THE CENTER OF COMPETITION

by Andrew Burt

I f you're selling a product, you're now selling trust.

That's thanks to two conflicting trends. One is our increasing reliance on software across nearly every dimension of our lives. It's for this reason that, among all *Fortune* 500 CEOs, a full 71% now claim they are running technology companies. The second is the inherent privacy and security vulnerabilities related to software itself.

As security and privacy pioneer Willis Ware once wryly declared, "The only computer that's completely secure is a computer that no one can use."

To navigate these two trends, companies across every vertical will need to prioritize data privacy and security, clearly demonstrate those priorities to consumers, and safeguard their relationships with customers by being fully honest about the dangers of data in the digital age.

That's where Olav Lysne, a Norwegian security researcher, and Apple CEO Tim Cook come in. While neither has much in common with the other, at least on the surface, they both illustrate how the future of technology—indeed, the future of business—is all about trust.

Let's start with Lysne.

A few years ago, the Norwegian government realized that it bought almost all of its critical technology from outside of Norway—think of the software that runs things like electric stations, water pumps, and cellular towers. Untrustworthy software might, for example, allow access to Norway's data in ways the government would disapprove—for example, to defraud the government by promising one thing and doing another, or to intentionally cease to function at a planned point in time.

These issues raised pressing national security questions: How could the government trust the technology it was increasingly reliant upon? What could Norway actually *do* to verify that it could depend on the software it was using?

In 2014, Lysne was tasked with leading a commission to answer these questions, an effort that culminated in a seminal book, *The Huawei and Snowden Questions.*

Lysne's answer: Norway's government simply could not verify as trustworthy the software it used. In fact, no one can. The very nature of our current software systems—the complexity underlying them, their supply chains, and more—makes it impossible to detect vulnerabilities intentionally inserted into software.

The sheer volume of code embedded into everyday objects, for example, is nearly impossible to review—the average car runs on an estimated 100 million lines of code, while Microsoft Office comprises up to 30 million lines of code. Meanwhile, the actual chips that make up circuit boards can be easily compromised themselves. These chips are composed of thousands, or in some cases millions, of gates; adding as few as 1,341 gates to just one chip has been shown to create a backdoor into an entire system.[1] The list of ways to compromise software is, as Lysne describes, seemingly endless.

This makes trust both the most important aspect of any commercial interaction and the hardest to measure. If we don't trust the maker, we simply don't know what it is we're getting. And because trust cannot be *proven*, it must be *signaled*—through branding, marketing, and more.

So what does Lysne have to do with Tim Cook?

Cook is one of the few corporate leaders to understand the implications of Lysne's conclusions. He has spent the past few years leading the charge in seeking to make trust the core of his company's public identity.

This helps explain why, for example, in 2016 Apple picked a series of fights with the federal government about access to its users' data while simultaneously staging a PR campaign around its actions.[2] This also is why, late in 2018, Cook publicly warned top European regulators of the dangers of the "data industrial complex" and called for new U.S. laws on data. And this is why Cook kicked off 2019 with an op-ed in *Time* magazine claiming to stand up for the rights of consumers who are simply "trying to win back their right to privacy."[3]

It doesn't hurt, of course, that this message also happens to undermine the ad-based revenue models of rivals such as Google and Facebook. But more broadly, Cook's campaign aligns with Apple's strategic interests. Indeed, it aligns with its own biggest long-term vulnerability.

That vulnerability is trust. While Cook cannot fix the problems Lysne identified—indeed, no one can—he can demonstrate that his company will do everything in its power to minimize them. He can make trust the core element of Apple's brand, which is exactly what he's been doing.

So how can other companies put these same lessons into practice?

To start with, trust must now be considered a key feature of every product containing software, no matter whether it is a purely digital product or a physical product containing software. In the consumer space, for example, studies have demonstrated that loss of trust can lead users to abandon a company or a product altogether. Some are even calling for a "return on trust" as a value proposition in and of itself.[4] As a result, security and privacy concerns can no longer take a back seat in the product development lifecycle—not simply because of the value of security and privacy alone, but for their business impact as well.

Second, clear and demonstrable processes must be put in place to illustrate the importance of data protection, both inside and outside every organization. What group is in charge of privacy? What group is in charge of security? Where do both enter the picture as product features are being developed or as new IT procurements are made, to pick just two examples? Organizations that can't answer these basic questions are failing to take data protection seriously—and are therefore primed to lose in the battle for consumer trust.

Once these processes are in place, companies can then signal their emphasis on protecting customer data to the outside world, just like Tim Cook. This is where marketing, branding, and public relations may get involved.

Last, and perhaps most important, companies and consumers alike must be honest about the risks we collectively face in the digital world. Because software systems are inherently vulnerable and the insights data might yield at scale cannot be predicted, no one should sugarcoat the dangers of digital technologies. Data breaches will occur, as will uses of data in ways that consumers can't foresee. Failures in the world of security and privacy are, in short, inevitable. To pretend otherwise is to undermine data-protection efforts from the start.

All signs indicate that companies beyond Apple are starting to take these lessons to heart, with over 200 now echoing Cook's calls for stronger federal privacy legislation in the United States. Are there other interests at work behind these calls? Surely. One national privacy regulation is easier to follow than 50 state laws.

But corporate America's increasing clamor to be viewed as security- and privacy-centric is no coincidence; it's a clear illustration of the increasing importance of trust. And that means we should expect all CEOs to be reading more Olav Lysne and to be acting more like Tim Cook.

TAKEAWAYS

We are increasingly reliant on networked software—and the privacy and security vulnerabilities that come with it—in nearly every aspect of our lives. Ultimately, the companies that customers trust most with their data will pull ahead of their competitors. Organizations that want to be seen as trustworthy need to prioritize data privacy and security, demonstrate those priorities to their customers, and safeguard their relationships with customers by being transparent about the threats to data:

✓ Trust can't be measured or proven, it must be signaled—through branding, marketing, and so on.

✓ Whether your company offers digital products or physical products that contain software, trust should be considered a key feature for every product.

✓ To demonstrate the importance of data protection, organizations must establish straightforward and evident processes.

✓ Companies and consumers must be honest and accept that the risks we face mean that security and privacy failures are inevitable.

NOTES

1. Samuel T. King et al., "Designing and Implementing Malicious Hardware," working paper, April 15, 2008, https://www.usenix.org /legacy/event/leet08/tech/full_papers/king/king_html/.

2. Nancy Gibbs and Lev Grossman, "Here's the Full Transcript of *Time*'s Interview with Apple CEO Tim Cook," *Time*, March 17, 2016, http://time.com/4261796/tim-cook-transcript/.

3. Tim Cook, "You Deserve Privacy Online. Here's How You Could Actually Get It," *Time* (Davos 2019), http://time.com/collection /davos-2019/5502591/tim-cook-data-privacy/.

4. Manish Bahl, "Return on Trust: The New Business Performance Indicator," Cognizant, July 21, 2016, https://www.cognizant.com /perspectives/return-on-trust-the-new-business-performance -indicator.

Adapted from content posted on hbr.org, March 4, 2019 (product #H04TMU).

PRIVACY AND CYBERSECURITY ARE CONVERGING

Here's Why That Matters for People and for Companies

by Andrew Burt

P rivacy issues have dominated headlines in recent years. These events are symptoms of larger, profound shifts in the world of data privacy and security that have major implications for how organizations think about and manage both.

So what exactly is changing?

Put simply, privacy and security are converging, thanks to the rise of big data and machine learning. What was once an abstract concept designed to protect expectations about our own data is now becoming more concrete, and more critical—on par with the threat of adversaries accessing our data without authorization.

More specifically, the threat of *unauthorized access* to our data used to pose the biggest danger to our digital selves—that was a world in which we worried about intruders attempting to get at data we wanted private. And it was a world in which privacy and security were largely separate functions, where privacy took a back seat to the more tangible concerns over security. Today, however, the biggest risk to our privacy and our security has become the threat of *unintended inferences*, due to the power of increasingly widespread machine learning techniques. Once we generate data, anyone who possesses enough of it can be a threat, posing new dangers to both our privacy and our security.

These inferences may, for example, threaten our anonymity—like when a group of researchers used machine learning techniques to identify authorship of written text based simply on patterns in language.[1] (Similar techniques have been used to identify software developers based simply on the code they've written.[2])

These inferences might reveal information about our political leanings—like when researchers used the prevalence of certain types of cars in Google's Street View image database to determine local political affiliations.[3]

Or these inferences might also indicate intimate details about our health—like when researchers used online search history to detect neurodegenerative disorders such as Alzheimer's.[4]

So what does a world look like when privacy and security are focused on preventing the same harms?

To start with, privacy will no longer be the merely immaterial or political concept it once was. Instead, privacy will begin to have substantial impacts on businesses' bottom lines—something we began to see in 2018. Facebook, for example, lost a whopping $119 billion in market capitalization in the wake of the Cambridge Analytica scandal because of concerns over privacy. Polls show that consumers are increasingly concerned about privacy issues. And governments around the world are reacting with new privacy legislation of their own.

Within organizations, this convergence also means that the once-clear line between privacy and security teams is beginning to blur—a trend that businesses in general, and security and privacy practitioners in particular, should embrace. From a practical perspective, this means that legal and privacy personnel will become more technical, and technical personnel will become more familiar with legal and compliance mandates. The idea of two distinct teams, operating independently of each other, will become a relic of the past.

And this means individuals and governments alike should no longer expect consent to play a meaningful role in protecting our privacy. Because the threat of unintended inferences reduces our ability to understand the value of our data, our expectations about our privacy—and therefore what we can meaningfully consent to—are becoming less consequential. Being *surprised* at the nature of the violation, in short, will become an inherent feature of future privacy and security harms.

This is precisely why the recent string of massive data breaches, from the Marriott breach that impacted 500 million guests to the Yahoo breach that affected 3 billion users, is so troubling. The problem isn't simply that unauthorized intruders accessed these records at a single point in time; the problem is all the unforeseen uses and all the intimate inferences that this volume of data can generate going forward. It is for this reason that legal scholars such as Oxford's Sandra Wachter are now proposing legal constraints around the ability to perform this type of pattern recognition at all.[5]

Once described by Supreme Court justice Louis Brandeis as "the right to be let alone," privacy is now best described as the ability to control data we cannot stop generating, giving rise to inferences we can't predict.

And because we create more and more data every day—an estimated 2.5 quintillion bytes of it—these issues will only become more pressing over time.

TAKEAWAYS

Thanks to the rise of big data and machine learning, privacy and security are converging. The largest threat is no longer unauthorized access to our data—it is the unintended, uncannily accurate inferences made by algorithms that are able to sift through and combine multiple sets of data:

✓ Consumers and government are taking note, by abandoning platforms they can't trust and introducing new privacy legislation.

✓ For organizations, this means security and privacy teams will have to work together more closely; legal and privacy personnel will become more technical, and technical personnel will become more familiar with legal and compliance mandates.

✓ For individuals and governments, this means consent will no longer play a meaningful role in protecting privacy.

NOTES

1. Arvind Narayanan et al., "On the Feasibility of Internet-Scale Author Identification," 2012 IEEE Symposium on Security and Privacy, May 2012, https://ieeexplore.ieee.org/document/6234420/authors#authors.

2. Aylin Caliskan et al., "When Coding Style Survives Compilation: De-anonymizing Programmers from Executable Binaries," Cornell University working paper, December 18, 2017, https://arxiv.org/abs/1512.08546.

3. Timnit Gebru et al., "Using Deep Learning and Google Street View to Estimate the Demographic Makeup of the US," *PNAS* 114, no. 50 (2017): 13108–13113.

4. Ryen W. White, P. Murali Doraiswamy, and Eric Horvitz, "Detecting Neurodegenerative Disorders from Web Search Signals," *Nature*, April 23, 2018, https://www.nature.com/articles/s41746-018-0016-6.

5. Sandra Wachter and Brent Mittelstadt, "A Right to Reasonable Inferences: Re-Thinking Data Protection Law in the Age of Big Data and AI," *Columbia Business Law Review*, September 13, 2018, https://papers.ssrn.com/sol3/papers.cfm?abstract_id=3248829.

Adapted from content posted on hbr.org, January 3, 2019 (product #H04PY8).

WHAT COUNTRIES AND COMPANIES CAN DO WHEN TRADE AND CYBERSECURITY OVERLAP

by Stuart Madnick, Simon Johnson, and Keman Huang

C ybersecurity as a key issue for trade policy is a relatively new development. In the last few years there
have been a number of news reports about various
governments' incorporating spyware, malware, or similar
programs into computer-based products that are exported

around the world. The governments typically have worked with private companies in their countries to do it. In the internet-of-things era, almost all products can be connected to the internet, and most of them can also be used for spying and other malicious activities. Furthermore, since data is considered a critical asset, services, from international banking to payment systems to consumer websites, are part of this too.

In late 2016 and 2017, for example, the voice-activated doll, My Friend Cayla, made headlines for its technology, which could be used to collect information on children or anyone in the room. In 2017 Germany banned the doll, alleging that it contained a surveillance device that violated the country's privacy regulations. Another famous example is the 2010 Stuxnet attack on the Natanz nuclear enrichment facility in Iran. It was accomplished by planting malware, including Stuxnet, into industrial control systems that were shipped to Iran, resulting in the destruction of many centrifuges.

Although trade conflicts involving the United States and China, or the United States and Russia, have received much attention in the press, cybersecurity-related trade conflict is a truly global phenomenon. As part of

---

The research reported herein was supported in part by the MIT Internet Research Policy Initiative, which is funded by the Hewlett Foundation, and Cybersecurity at MIT Sloan, which is funded by a consortium of organizations.

our initial research on this topic, we identified 33 cases of a country blocking the import of a product or service due to cybersecurity concerns. In each one, different circumstances and actions led to different outcomes. The cases involved 19 countries all over the world, and in the future it's likely that these kinds of trade conflicts will involve almost all developed countries.

Since it is not feasible to thoroughly examine the software, firmware, and hardware of every single product, what should countries and companies do to prevent cyber intrusions? One seemingly obvious approach is to exclude from import potentially dangerous products from questionable countries. But this approach requires identifying which products are dangerous and which countries are questionable—a formidable task. And such restrictions can quickly become policies, with implications for international trade and the world economy.

Countries and companies need to consider their options. At present, there is no framework for understanding and categorizing the cybersecurity concerns involved in trade. Without a clear understanding, governments may implement policies that result in cyber conflicts, while businesses will struggle to keep up with how cybersecurity concerns and restrictions are evolving. We have developed a framework to systematically organize these cases, basing it on our in-depth interviews with domain experts.

What Options Do Countries Have?

There are various possible actions that governments can take. Each of the following should be carefully considered:

Do nothing: Governments can accept the potential risk of a cybersecurity situation and choose to ignore it. In 2004, for example, the German Federal Intelligence Service (BND) discovered that the hardware company NetBotz, then based in the United States, was selling security cameras with a backdoor that sent videos to U.S. military servers. The BND did not disclose that fact until 2015, only after a magazine had discovered and revealed the situation.

Develop import trade barriers: Some nations will take actions to implement trade policies or regulations that will directly restrict the import of international trades, such as Germany's banning of the My Friend Cayla doll.

Restrict government procurement: Governments can prohibit the use and purchase of certain products. For example:

- The United States banned government and military systems from using Kaspersky Lab security software and drones made by Chinese company DJI.

- China removed networking equipment from Cisco Systems and security software from McAfee and Citrix Systems from its government procurement lists.

Develop norms of behavior: Countries can agree to not engage in certain types of behavior, such as when the United States and China agreed not to conduct the cybertheft of intellectual property for commercial purposes.[1]

Amplify the conflict: On the other hand, some nations can choose an opposite option and escalate the conflict. The United States and Russia, for example, have developed a tense relationship, which has been referred to as the "Cold War 2.0."

What Options Do Companies Have?

Although government actions and concerns are often more visible, companies need not play a passive role. They can anticipate these concerns and take actions to reduce or mitigate the consequences. There are various options available:

Recommend action: For example, on August 9, 2017, 10 major cybersecurity companies in the United States wrote to Robert Lighthizer, the U.S. trade representative, to urge that he "incorporate cybersecurity trade issues in the upcoming modernization of the North American Free Trade Agreement (NAFTA)."

Acquiesce: As noted earlier, Germany took action against the My Friend Cayla doll due to concerns about privacy. The company acquiesced and stopped selling it in Germany.

Compromise: Telegram, the end-to-end encrypted messaging app, was threatened with a ban in Russia, so the company agreed to register under the new Russian data protection laws; however, it will not store citizens' information on Russian servers. As another example, Google exited the Chinese market in 2010 to avoid having to censure its search results to meet Chinese government rules. The company has recently decided to reenter, with modest changes to its search engine operation. It is not yet clear that this compromise will be accepted by both parties.

Avoid: Typical examples include Google's withdrawal from China and Huawei's withdrawal of its network hardware products from the United States in 2014. The latter occurred after the products were removed from U.S. government procurement lists and private telecommunications companies were advised not to purchase Huawei products.

Defy: An organization may challenge or attack cybersecurity regulations. For example, in 2016 LinkedIn challenged the Russian data protection laws, stating that it would not move Russian user data to the country. As a result, Russia blocked LinkedIn in 2017.

Collaborate: Finally, organizations can choose to work with countries to mitigate the negative impact of regulations, or even to be involved in the regulation-making process. An example of this is how Huawei has worked with the U.K. government.

In 2011, worried about potential spying, the U.S. government rejected a bid from Huawei to build a new national wireless network for first responders. This was followed by further government restrictions on Huawei. Finally, in 2014, Huawei decided to exit the U.S. market.

The United Kingdom, on the other hand, does use the company's technology in national infrastructure. In 2010 it opened the Huawei Cyber Security Evaluation Centre to monitor concerns about the technology's use. This was followed in early 2014 by the establishment of an oversight board, which every year releases a report about any risks from Huawei's involvement in the United Kingdom's critical networks. It should be noted, however, that the oversight board's 2018 report raised serious new concerns about Huawei's technology and the security risks it could pose to U.K. security.

As the digital economy continues to develop, cybersecurity will play a critical role in international trade. Instead of considering security only a regulation issue, governments need to consider ways to avoid unnecessary confrontations, and organizations should become proactively involved to address concerns and influence policy to improve outcomes for everyone.

TAKEAWAYS

Since it's impossible to adequately examine the software, firmware, and hardware of every single product that enters a country, countries and companies need to consider their options when it comes to preventing cyber intrusions:

✓ Governments have various actions they can elect to take, from opting to accept potential risk and do nothing, to developing trade policies to restrict the importing of certain types of products from certain countries, to developing norms by agreeing on what types of behavior they will and won't engage in.

✓ Companies affected by government intervention into trade (whether on the import or export side) have a range have a range of choices, from recommending action or policy changes to their government, acquiescing to government mandates, trying to find compromises, challenging regulations, or collaborating and working with countries to mitigate the negative impact or help create regulations.

NOTE

1. Everett Rosenfeld, "US-China Agree to Not Conduct Cybertheft of Intellectual Property," CNBC, September 25, 2015, https://www.cnbc.com/2015/09/25/us-china-agree-to-not-conduct-cybertheft-of-intellectual-property-white-house.html.

Adapted from content posted on hbr.org, January 4, 2019 (product #H04QA4).

AI IS THE FUTURE OF CYBERSECURITY, FOR BETTER AND FOR WORSE

by Roman V. Yampolskiy

I n the near future, as artificial intelligence (AI) systems become more capable, we will begin to see more automated and increasingly sophisticated social engineering attacks. The rise of AI-enabled cyberattacks is expected to cause an explosion of network penetrations, personal data thefts, and an epidemic-level spread of intelligent computer viruses. Ironically, our best hope to defend against AI-enabled hacking is by using AI. But this is very likely to lead to an AI arms race, the consequences of which may be very troubling in the long term, especially as big government actors join the cyber wars.

My research is at the intersection of AI and cybersecurity. In particular, I am researching how we can protect AI systems from bad actors, as well as how we can protect people from failed or malevolent AI. This work falls into a larger framework of AI safety, efforts to create AI that is exceedingly capable but also safe and beneficial.

A lot has been written about problems that might arise with the arrival of "true AI," either as a direct impact of such inventions or because of a programmer's error. However, intentional malice in design and AI hacking have not been addressed to a sufficient degree in the scientific literature. It's fair to say that when it comes to dangers from a purposefully unethical intelligence, anything is possible. According to Nick Bostrom's orthogonality thesis, an AI system can potentially have any combination of intelligence and goals. Such goals can be introduced either through the initial design or through hacking, or introduced later, in case of an off-the-shelf software— "just add your own goals." Consequently, depending on whose bidding the system is doing (governments, corporations, sociopaths, dictators, military industrial complexes, terrorists, and so on), it may attempt to inflict damage that's unprecedented in the history of human-kind—or that's perhaps inspired by previous events.

Even today, AI can be used to defend and to attack cyber infrastructure, as well as to increase the attack surface that hackers can target, that is, the number of ways for hackers to get into a system. In the future, as AIs increase in capability, I anticipate that they will first reach and then overtake humans in all domains of performance, as we have already seen with games like chess and Go and are now seeing with important human tasks such as investing and driving. It's important for business leaders to understand how that future situation will differ from our current concerns and what to do about it.

If one of today's cybersecurity systems fails, the damage can be unpleasant, but it's tolerable in most cases: Someone loses money or privacy. But for human-level AI (or above), the consequences could be catastrophic. A single failure of a superintelligent AI (SAI) system could cause an existential risk event—an event that has the potential to damage human well-being on a global scale. The risks are real, as evidenced by the fact that some of the world's greatest minds in technology and physics, including Stephen Hawking, Bill Gates, and Elon Musk, have expressed concerns about the potential for AI to evolve to a point where humans could no longer control it.

When one of today's cybersecurity systems fails, we typically get another chance to get it right, or at least to do better next time. But with an SAI safety system, failure or success is a binary situation: Either we have a safe, controlled SAI or we don't. The goal of cybersecurity in general is to reduce the number of successful attacks on a system; the goal of SAI safety, in contrast, is to make sure no attacks succeed in bypassing the safety mechanisms in place. The rise of brain-computer interfaces, in particular, will create a dream target for human and AI-enabled hackers. And brain-computer interfaces are not so futuristic—they're already being used in medical devices and gaming, for example. If successful, attacks on brain-computer interfaces would compromise not only critical information such as social security numbers or bank account numbers but also our deepest dreams, preferences, and secrets. The potential exists to create unprecedented new dangers for personal privacy, free speech, equal opportunity, and any number of human rights.

Business leaders are advised to familiarize themselves with the cutting edge of AI safety and security research, which at the moment is sadly similar to the state of cybersecurity in the 1990s, and our current situation with the lack of security for the internet of things. Armed with more knowledge, leaders can rationally consider how the addition of AI to their product or service will enhance user experiences, while weighing the costs of potentially subjecting users to additional data breaches and possible dangers. Hiring a dedicated AI safety expert may be an important next step, as most cybersecurity experts are not trained in anticipating or preventing attacks against intelligent systems. I am hopeful that ongoing research will bring additional solutions for safely incorporating AI into the marketplace.

TAKEAWAYS

As AI systems become more capable, automated and sophisticated cyberattacks will rise. And the best defense for these cyberattacks? More AI.

✓ A single failure of a superintelligent AI system could cause a risk event so significant it could have the potential to damage human well-being on a global scale.

✓ The rise of brain-computer interfaces creates a dream target for both human and AI-enabled hackers: targets from critical information such as social security numbers to our deepest dreams and secrets.

Adapted from content posted on hbr.org, May 8, 2017 (product #H03NES).

About the Contributors

SCOTT BERINATO is a senior editor at *Harvard Business Review* and the author of *Good Charts: The HBR Guide to Making Smarter, More Persuasive Data Visualizations* (Harvard Business Review Press, 2016) and *Good Charts Workbook* (Harvard Business Review Press, 2019). Follow him on Twitter @scottberinato.

ALEX BLAU is a vice president at ideas42 and coauthor of *Deep Thought: A Cybersecurity Story*, a true-crime-style novella that dramatizes human behavioral threats in cybersecurity. He applies insights from behavioral science to solve design and decision-making challenges in a broad array of domains. His current foci at ideas42 are in the areas of cybersecurity, privacy, public safety, and product design.

ANDY BOCHMAN is senior grid strategist, national and homeland security, Idaho National Laboratory.

BILL BOURDON is president and co-owner at Bateman Group (www.bateman-group.com/). Learn more about his work at bateman-group.com; follow him on Twitter @bbourdon.

ANDREW BURT is chief privacy officer and legal engineer at Immuta.

J. YO-JUD CHENG is an assistant professor of business administration at the University of Virginia's Darden School of Business.

DANTE DISPARTE is the founder and CEO of Risk Cooperative. He is the coauthor of the book *Global Risk Agility and Decision Making* (2016).

CHRIS FURLOW is president and CEO of the Texas Bankers Association and a member of the Texas Cybersecurity Council.

BORIS GROYSBERG is the Richard P. Chapman Professor of Business Administration at Harvard Business School, faculty affiliate at the HBS gender initiative, and the coauthor, with Michael Slind, of *Talk, Inc.* (Harvard Business Review Press, 2012). Follow him on Twitter @bgroysberg.

JASON J. HOGG is CEO of Aon Cyber Solutions, which helps organizations manage the financial and technical aspects of cyber risks.

KEMAN HUANG is a research scientist at the MIT Sloan School of Management, where he works on cybersecurity management and policy, innovation ecosystems, and big data analysis.

SIMON JOHNSON is the Ronald A. Kurtz (1954) Professor of Entrepreneurship at the MIT Sloan School of Management, where he is also head of the global economics and management group and chair of the Sloan Fellows MBA program committee.

STUART MADNICK is the John Norris Maguire (1960) Professor of Information Technologies at the MIT Sloan School of Management, Professor of engineering systems in the MIT School of Engineering, and director of cybersecurity at MIT Sloan (CAMS): The Interdisciplinary Consortium for Improving Critical Infrastructure Cybersecurity. He has been active in the cybersecurity field since coauthoring the book *Computer Security* in 1979.

MATT PERRY is senior graphics editor at *Harvard Business Review*. Explore his work at mattperrygraphics.com.

MAARTEN VAN HORENBEECK is a security manager who formerly led Amazon's threat intelligence team and held security roles at Google and Microsoft. He's currently vice president of security engineering at Fastly.

ROMAN V. YAMPOLSKIY is a tenured associate professor in the department of computer engineering and computer science at the Speed School of Engineering, University of Louisville. He is the founding and current director of the university's cybersecurity lab and an author of many books, including *Artificial Superintelligence: A Futuristic Approach.* Follow him on Twitter @romanyam.

Index

Is Your Business Ready for the Future?

If you enjoyed this book and want more on today's pressing business topics, turn to other books in the **Insights You Need** series from *Harvard Business Review*. Featuring HBR's latest thinking on topics critical to your company's success—from Blockchain and Cybersecurity to AI and Agile—each book will help you explore these trends and how they will impact you and your business in the future.

FOR MORE VISIT HBR.ORG/BOOKS

The most important management ideas all in one place.

We hope you enjoyed this book from *Harvard Business Review*. Now you can get even more with HBR's 10 Must Reads Boxed Set. From books on leadership and strategy to managing yourself and others, this 6-book collection delivers articles on the most essential business topics to help you succeed.

HBR's 10 Must Reads Series

The definitive collection of ideas and best practices on our most sought-after topics from the best minds in business.

- Change Management
- Collaboration
- Communication
- Emotional Intelligence
- Innovation
- Leadership
- Making Smart Decisions

- Managing Across Cultures
- Managing People
- Managing Yourself
- Strategic Marketing
- Strategy
- Teams
- The Essentials

hbr.org/mustreads

Buy for your team, clients, or event.
Visit hbr.org/bulksales for quantity discount rates.

www.ingramcontent.com/pod-product-compliance
Lightning Source LLC
LaVergne TN
LVHW092009050326
832904LV00002B/32